'There's an entire generation ( who ought to read this book, for selves and hopefully forgive themselves for believing every lie ever told about them and every expectation ever imposed on them simply by virtue of their having a vagina. Fife's candour in telling her story with such searing honesty is both exciting and empowering – her voice is an important one in our collective journey as women of colour to healing and, ultimately, acceptance of ourselves just as we are. *Ougat* is breathtakingly frank, unapologetically honest, and refreshingly relatable.'

– **Sara-Jayne King**, author of *Killing Karoline* and host on Cape Talk

'What a shock to the system Shana Fife's *Ougat* is, as she lays bare the multiple layers of her gritty vulnerability. Fife takes one into the heart of the customary uncle swagger and complicit auntyness of being and right into the convoluted realities of defiant youth. Always battling on, with her wounds oozing riotous emotions, psycho-social toxicity, battered physicality and guilt-tripped spirituality, *Ougat*'s odd-ball fixations are bound to leave you catching flies as the jaw drops, laughing insanely or wiping away tears of empathy. Yoh! What a read.'

– **Bronwyn Davids**, author of *Lansdowne Dearest*

'How do you manage to write a book in which you describe your deepest secrets, your most intimate thoughts, your darkest hours and your greatest humiliation in fine detail and honesty? Shana Fife captures all the darkness from her body, psyche and life with fearless honesty and transparency. I am relieved that in our country we have brave women like her who can use her writing skills to give a voice, not only to her story, but to thousands of other women who experience abuse daily. *Ougat* is masterfully written. It is one of the most important books of our time.'

– **Frazer Barry**, award-winning theatre practitioner,
writer and musician

'Rich, rewarding and revealing . . . A rip-roaring, no-punches-pulled account of a life from someone with a hell of a lot to say – and the means to do so.'

– **Francois Bloemhof**, bestselling author

# Ougat

From a hoe into a housewife
and then some

*by*

# Shana Fife

Jonathan Ball Publishers
Johannesburg • Cape Town • London

Originally published in South Africa in 2018 by
JONATHAN BALL PUBLISHERS
A division of Media24 (Pty) Ltd
PO Box 33977
Jeppestown
2043

ISBN 978-1-77619-082-9
eBook ISBN 978-1-77619-083-6

Every effort has been made to trace the copyright holders and to
obtain their permission for the use of copyright material. The publishers
apologise for any errors or omissions and would be grateful to be notified of any
corrections that should be incorporated in future editions of this book.

Website: www.jonathanball.co.za
Twitter: www.twitter.com/JonathanBallPub
Facebook: www.facebook.com/JonathanBallPublishers

Cover by publicide
Design and typesetting by Nazli Jacobs

Set in Versailles

This book is dedicated to
my husband and children,
and my mom and dad.
You all are my whole heart –
I would go through it all again
to have what I have now, in all of you.

And it's also dedicated to God, of course.

# Contents

# Chapter 1

# 'Aspoestertjie' and other innocent words

The very first rule that you are given as a Coloured child who has a vagina is that no one is allowed to touch it. Ever. Even with your consent. Especially not with your consent. The revelation of your pussy is prohibited and will bring shame to your father, to your brother and most importantly, to God. Trying to not disappoint God is a massive weight to bear for a five-year-old. But the weight of male approval is just as heavy. Even at this tender age, every man in your family will tell you about how – when you are old enough to have a boyfriend, which is never – they will kill him, mafia-style, as a warning to all other men that you are from a respectable, male-dominated tribe.

This, of course, is a testament to the fact that all men are trash and all men know that they are trash ... These men are willing to protect the women they know from the other trash, but only to protect their own honour, by protecting her honour. It is all a convoluted fuck-up.

Regardless, you will remain a virgin until your wedding day, while your family completely ignores the irony that you may actually need to date someone before they know you well enough to propose. The proposal is the goal. Every step you take from birth to the ultimate marriage proposal is an audition for a man to choose you, like an object in the shop, or a career, or a Pokémon. And of course, along the way, everyone will ask you when you are getting married, but will judge you for having male suitors; and yes, there will be rumours of your compromised chastity.

Even at high school, when you realise that you have sexual desires just like the boys do, the boys at your school will only talk to you if you put out. But they will only date you if you pretend you don't put out. Then you must put out. But you mustn't like it. Unless they ask if you like it. To which you will mumble a shy, ambiguous non-response because you are so fucking confused at what is happening that it is safer to go with the flow and not look absolutely inexperienced – or too comfortable.

But your sexual identity and desires will morph and grow, continuously in conflict with your morality, until you are nothing but an obsessively masturbating, churchgoing, virginal daddy's girl with two illegitimate children.

My name is Shana Fife and this is my story.

As of writing this, I am 30 years old. A series of unfortunate, yet retrospectively somehow necessary events has led me to my very unconventional calling: telling people about my vagina. I also speak about abuse. Sexual abuse. Gender-based abuse. And everything else that makes people roll their eyes and whisper 'fucking feminazi'.

Professionally, I write for corporates and create content that is digestible to the masses. I specialise in lifestyle articles about decor and diets and 'What to do when you're having an asthma attack', but that's just a cover-up for what I really do: I am a blogger in the vagina and feminism market. Even in 2021 the term 'blogger' is synonymous with 'influencer' or 'wannabe writer'. So, when I introduce myself I mostly mumble 'I'm a journalist' when I am asked what I do for money.

I'm also a certified failure to my community, my orthodox Catholic Coloured family and Jesus. (I suppose we should use the past tense here; I got married in 2017 so now I'm golden.) But mine is a story of the sum of the things that made up the Coloured community in the 80s and 90s, the tale of a child who wasn't quite sure of where she fitted into society or her very diverse family. It's a story about a constant battle of choosing between who I was, who I was expected to be and who I wanted to be.

And guilt and conditioning.

Oh, and how I got into an abusive relationship that nearly fucking killed me.

But let's get back to this thing of failure.

In 2014 I found myself three years out of journalism school. I was broke and alone and had just given birth to my second illegitimate child.

Second. Illegitimate. Child.

I hate that term: illegitimate.

### Illegitimate
/ˌɪlɪˈdʒɪtɪmət/
Adjective
1. *not authorized by the law; not in accordance with accepted standards or rules.*

As if the child isn't real unless you're married to a man.

I was also in the throes of leaving Lyle. I was living back at my parents' home, in a single room with both of my kids – my son Sidney-Jonah and my daughter, Lyle's daughter, Syria-Rose. On one bed. Amidst boxes and extra cupboards and things. A storage facility, really. My life had taken another nosedive and I wasn't seeing any hope at the end of the tunnel this time.

I remember certain parts of that year distinctly, but there are days and weeks that seem blurry. Some things I have successfully blocked out, while other memories linger unwanted and visit me at 3am when my house and mind are too quiet.

And many such thoughts, even almost six years later, are of Lyle and all the things I let him do to me, to my body and to my mind.

I had been so defeated and dehumanised, I had no skin left on my face. I was lonely, disappointed by who I was and how I had become her.

One day, in the emotional whirlwind that was 2014, I sat down, defeated. Angry. Angry at my life. Angry at myself. Angry at my vagina, which seemed to be at the centre of all my problems. How had I fallen pregnant so many times? Why had no one sat me down and explained contraception, sexual desire and sperm to me? Was I the only one who didn't listen in Life Orientation? Surely women should constantly be teaching other women about sex? Am I just hornier than other women? Am I a whore? Am I an idiot for letting someone beat me to a pulp, rape me and still come near my children? Am I now spoiled for all mankind? A decent man would never hitch his wagon to my calibre of woman.

And most importantly, the question that would forever change my life: do other women feel the same way I do?

I sat down at my parents' dining room table and looked over the entirety of Pelican Heights, out over Strandfontein Beach to the ocean – and used the only marketable skill I had. I wrote. For no one. For myself. I wrote a short blog about having my card declined while buying milk or something. I just needed to vent. I didn't have friends to lose. I didn't have anyone's respect to lose. There was a long battle with myself about what was appropriate to write about. A push-pull between what was embarrassing, what made me sound good and what was true. The line between authenticity and self-deprecation became thinner the more I delved deeper into what was really happening and into who I really was. And when I posted it, I remember closing my laptop and going to the park next to my house with my children. I sat there holding Syria on my lap and watched Sidney play. And I cried. Not wildly or dramatically. I just sat there as the tears streamed down my face while Sidney, oblivious to the failure his mother was, played happily on the merry-go-round. I didn't know it yet, but from that day on, my life would do a 180.

I am getting ahead of things. We will get back to this story. We will get back to Lyle. We will get back to my pregnancies, my fall and my eventual rise. I promise this book will have all of the elements that make for a real Coloured skinnerstorie.

Perhaps I should answer the first question you probably have: who is Lyle and why is he significant? Of course, my memoir needs to centre around how I was affected by a man, right? Why else would anyone want to read it? Women aren't fucking interesting. Books about women are about boring shit like eating and praying and loving.

Well, this memoir is about how a man affected my life. How 'men' as a concept, particularly in the Coloured culture, has affected my life since I was a child. It speaks of how what is cliché – but still toxic – masculinity can shape and trap a woman from the cot to the cot (because our whole purpose, from when we are babies, is to eventually have our own babies).

But I start this book with him at the forefront because Lyle was the turning point in my life, or at least the catalyst for what would be the start of my mental and spiritual awakening. He was the first real boyfriend of my adult life and the more I think about it, my first encounter with evil.

13

I met Lyle when I was 21. We started out as friends, but the relationship quickly turned into a master–slave relationship. I endured beatings, rape and emotional destruction under his reign, and yet my story is by no means unique to my gender, to my race or to the world. I will share the sordid details nonetheless, on the off chance that it is a cautionary tale that saves at least one woman – on one condition: that it is understood that even though Lyle is the main subject of my life thus far, he is not the main character. I am.

And he is not the only part of my story.

# Chapter 2

# A brief herstory

To really understand why I ended up tied by the vagina to a cretin from the underworld, I need to look at where I come from. As a young woman, I aspired to be like the unhappy, but married, women in my circle. There were exceptions like fun aunties and independent cousins, but I remember mostly pitying the women who hadn't been lucky enough to find a man to tame them. From my peripheral viewpoint as a child it seemed that married women looked at single women with a mixture of disgust, pity and jealousy. Very confusing for my newly emerging sense of self. I had a sponge for a mind and it soaked up every sentiment expressed by the people I was told to look up to or else. Observing from my low angle, I was aware that men and boys were exempt from common decency – and that even though 'boys will be boys' and women were nurturers, matured faster and were fixers, men were destined to rule.

It made sense, but it didn't. But it did.

As a child, I was privy to the interesting dynamic between boys and girls and men and women that only Cape Coloured kids will understand. You only need to attend one wedding at a civic centre and see the women anxiously waiting for mediocre, drunk men to ask them to jazz to understand the entirety of heterosexuality in my community. But like I said, admitting that I was aware of anything above my age level – or expected chastity level – would mean that I was 'fast and forward'. I preferred to dumb myself down to the point of pretending to be shy about trivial things, rather than let people know I had found my own vagina. And that I thought that they, even at 20 years older than me, were fucking stupid.

Even as a seven-year-old I noticed the disparities between men and women. But I knew very well I was to keep my observations to myself, no matter how accurate they were. There was a certain way I was to behave, or I would be 'in the eyes'. In my very first memory of my extended family in our Woodlands home, my mother's brothers and sisters and their children are all gathered to celebrate my grandparents' fiftieth anniversary. My cousin Louis and I were the youngest children of my ma's daughters. Apparently, that was significant to these old farts, so it was our duty – our honour – to present my grandparents with their gift: a box-shaped colour TV. Everyone was so excited at the idea of presenting this monstrosity to them. Like with any Coloured affair that needed planning and coordination, everyone was also angry. (My family doesn't do well under pressure. Every emotion can somehow slide into anger.) Regardless, after the half-assed speeches and an awkward pause for me and my cousin to unveil the gift, I remember hearing my uncle mutter a drunken, 'Lat Louis dit oop maak – hy's die boy.' I honestly had no idea what that meant. Even my baby brain knew that there was no logical link between the two sentences – why should Louis open it, just because he was the boy? But everyone else seemed to understand, leaving me doubting my own judgement.

After an anticlimactic unveiling, it was time for the food. I cannot remember what was on the menu, but I am willing to bet it was biryani and chicken something. It was always chicken something. And let me tell you, the dishing up always went the exact same way. The women would spend hours in the kitchen cleaning and cooking and preparing treats, while the men did something enjoyable in the other parts of the house. Whether the men indulged in a sports match on TV or sat and had a few drinks in the yard, they were always having a good time while they waited for the food. Once the food was prepared and laid out on the table, the women would stand back as the men were given first pickings of the dishes: 'Lat die mansmense skep.'

Men dished up first. This was the rule. And on the odd occasion that a woman was at the front of the line, she was probably dishing up for her incapacitated husband.

Following the meals, women would hurriedly excuse themselves from the dining table to make their way to the kitchen again, this time to clean and pack away the dishes and leftovers, and to make way for the cakes and tea that they would prepare. As the men recovered from a hard day's worth of doing absolutely fuck all.

But it always seemed like the women were happy to be on their toes, parading around for the men. Instead of having their own identities, their entire self-worth was based on how well they served their husbands, on how other women, and men, saw them serving their husbands. The manlier their wifely servitude made their men look, the more accomplished the women felt.

Come back to the present with me for a second.

The parameters for being a woman have both changed and remained the same in the minefieldesque online landscape we live in. Yes, we are making up words now; just go with it.

These days, you are allowed to be a liberated woman. It is encouraged, mostly. As long as your femininity comes with a comfortable sexuality. A calm sexuality that isn't aggressive.

You may embrace your vagina, but in a demure, shy way. Even if you aren't shy, pretend to be, it's cute. You know, fragile masculinity cannot handle women speaking of their own vaginas as if they are proud or something – only men are allowed such liberties: to speak of our vaginas. Any liberties, really. Liberty is only a lady, because she was created for the enjoyment of straight men.

Though in another twist of irony, if you do decide that you are tired of years of oppression and want to use your lady bits for your own pleasure, you have to tell everyone about it. If you don't, you might find yourself, instead of fighting the patriarchy, fighting those who fight the patriarchy. They tell you exactly why you are complicit in the oppression of women – but they do this by not allowing you to be a woman outside of their parameters. Instead of identifying their own internal struggles with authority, their own failed relationships with men and with themselves, they force you into their definition of liberation. Oppressively liberating their idea of you and who you should be into only one type of freedom: the freedom to shout vulgarly about your pussy, even if you don't particularly want to.

But the alternative is whispering it quietly and coyly so that the men who know you are proud of your silent, ladylike take on this New Aged feminism bullshit.

You cannot simply exist as an equal to everyone, with sexuality just being a normal part of who you are. It must either be only who you are, or definitely who you are not.

Of course, marriage is no longer the goal, unless you want it to be; but other women should definitely aim for it, because you are pretty sure they are just responding to loneliness with fake independence. Your independence is different, though; you like being alone – until you find a man who is worthy of you, or will put up with your absolute lack of personality and your unwillingness to compromise on anything. So that your feminist friends and woke men compadres can be proud of how you are actively breaking the mould. So that you can instead be the bully and right every prejudice – by cancelling anyone who disagrees with you, believing every woman who has a claim against any man and throwing people into jail for merely defending them-selves (unless the said offenders are people you know personally: then it is okay to empathise and work on a case-by-case basis). Never back down, but also accept duality with an open chakra. Align your goddamn chi, or decalcify your pineal gland by avoid-ing fluoride, but for the love of God, hygiene – you're a lady. Nobody likes a smelly woman. Jy lê lanks 'n man.

And if you do want to get married, you can pretend to agree to 'be submissive' in your vows, just for the show (because being too liberated isn't conducive to being wifey material – and true liberation does not exist off Facebook, right? Activism means sharing the right memes to make a difference. But we still like piel in real life). It is fine to be a wild feminist until a man finds it endearing, but once you are married you can stop the charade: you have made your point, love. Now you must be as liberated as your husband allows you to be and constantly give him props for his open-mindedness, or he might just say you can't be liber-ated anymore. You wouldn't want to embarrass him. Especially if he allows you to be yourself and doesn't expect you to do 'all the wife things', because he takes your goals into consideration. What a legend.

Get that education, girl. Have that corporate career – but re-member to be home before your husband gets there so that you can feed him, bath the kids and sex him. Because he is a good man, who helps you (with chores that should actually be split equally, because you know, he lives there too). Make your feelings known, but don't complain or get flustered. You look pretty when you smile.

Thank God we have progressed from that 1950s way of thinking. Life as a woman is so much simpler now. Also, men are openly murdering us at an exponential rate, so there's that.

I have entered this arena, fully prepared to be cancelled for having an opinion. It comes with the territory.

But I digress. The way women are believed to be only there for masculine pleasure is abuse in my opinion. Full-on abuse of an entire gender, masked as fucking tradition.

And it goes even deeper than that. Coloured children are abused under the same guise too – one that is ingrained in us as discipline and respect.

Abuse is an interesting concept, a multi-layered one. I envision it to be an iceberg. The tip of the iceberg is the outright swearing and violence which acts as a means to call it out and act appalled, but beneath the surface the wide, fat ass of abuse is so hidden that we only acknowledge the tip and let everything else slide. I think that all of us are a little bit abused. From childhood, we are so desensitised by 'acceptable abuse' that is hidden under the surface of everyday interaction, and by 'cultural norms', that we eventually stop noticing the massive bottom of the iceberg. I really suck at metaphors.

As Coloured children, we are taught that our bodies belong to our parents. We are given hidings when we step out of line. This is accepted by all the other adults around us and applauded as a 'good upbringing'. I think this instills the belief that when we step out of line, we deserve to be physically assaulted as long as the person doing it has authority in the relationship. Parent/child. Teacher/learner. Husband/wife.

My mother was a disciplinarian. But, in her defense, the community and family she came from likened sparing the rod to dooming the child. I never understood why certain offences in my home held a corporal punishment, but what my developing brain did understand was that everyone who knew that my mom was disciplining me in this way was okay with it. It wasn't the same as when people abused their kids. The difference is still lost on me, but that is a whole other can of worms. It is not my place to set the moral parameters for just how much someone may harm their own child. Though perhaps, as a community, we should set new boundaries and weed out the abusers from behind the cultural safety nets. In fact, shouldn't those safety nets be for the children? The damage is so deep that even now, children who were beaten out of 'love and discipline' will as adults defend their parents. Perhaps having to accept that our heroes are fallible is harder than standing up for ourselves against years of tradition. Because then we will need to be introspective and cease hitting our own kids, an honour we have been waiting for as if it is a rite of passage – our hard-earned, God-given turn to be the bullies.

In the Coloured community I grew up in, all of my friends and acquaintances got hidings from their parents. Being grounded was for white children. We didn't come from families who could afford to give us an allowance, never mind withhold it from us as punishment. Coloured laaities were moered (at least, those of us from respectable homes). We would be so desensitised to violence that we would all share the stories of how our parents hit us and laugh at whoever's story was the most erg. Besides, we saw people die in the roads we lived in more often than we should have. Complaining about a few warme, deserved klappe was childish; and the last thing a Coloured child wanted to be was 'like a laaitie'.

'Remember that day your taani moered you with a bag of rollers?' I would ask my friend and laugh. 'Yoh, she hit you in your poes! You were kak cross.' And my friend would laugh with me, because the offences were just part of our lives. We would laugh them off, as a coping mechanism, I see now. It was also comforting that all of us could relate. It was hard to see the line between what was a 'normal hiding', or when your friend was in trouble. We weren't really allowed to speak out of our homes, though, so we couldn't report anything that we saw that we thought wasn't okay. It wasn't our job to think, not until we were out of our parents' houses, under our own roofs.

An incident in my teens would affect my perception of both what was allowed to happen between parent and child, and within a relationship that I didn't know yet. It altered and perverted what I thought a woman's role should be.

One night, a friend of mine had a party at her home. I can't remember what the party was for but all of my friends from the area were there, and we had alcohol and weed seeping from our pores. Surrounded by the boys from my neighbourhood, it felt so lekker to be young and thin and have long hair. We were drinking beers and laughing at mediocre jokes told by unsuccessful young boys who, unbeknownst to us then, would turn into heroin addicts with no teeth in our thirties. The ignorance and bliss of youth is unmatched.

When the dop was sufficiently trekked through our young bodies, we decided to walk each other home. We all lived five minutes away from each other, so naturally, in line with the law of Coloured neighbourhood kids, we made sure to walk everyone to their doors – most feminine first, with the roughest of the lot making a run for it alone in the dark last. As we exited the party, my friend's dad was waiting outside the house.

Now, to give you context; he was the dad that we were all scared of – he crossed the line that made us feel endangered. We gave him the most respect though, because he commanded it. He instilled the most fear – and was therefore by default the authority – the alpha dad. A military man in his youth, he had married my friend's mom when she was a teenager. This was apparently an achievement for her, even though she went on to be a prisoner of war in her own home. She had three children from him and wasn't allowed to work or learn to drive. He was a provider to a fault. Removing his wife's rights, under the guise of taking care of her needs. Unwelcome help is also abuse, but beneath that calm water . . .

When we saw him standing outside at the party, we knew he was there for his daughter. She was in trouble. She was the eldest of all of us. Already 20, but with the earliest curfew. I had mentioned her limited liberties to many adults before, but I was always met with disgust at how ungrateful she was. She was a Coloured child, from a family that had married parents – she had a dad who took care of her financially – what difference were a few rules, or a few black eyes? We wouldn't even understand the implications of having no freedom as a child, then being expected to run your own life as an adult until much, much later.

I can still feel my jaw tighten in anxiety when I recall him spotting me as I exited the party. He asked me where she was. For anonymity, we will call her Felicia.

'Shana, is Felicia daar binne?' He asked me about her because he was most familiar with me, because he and my mother were allies in discipline. I tried to straighten up my intoxicated spine. Because I came from a disciplinarian home, he trusted me the most.

'Hello uncle, no she isn't, she uh . . .' I remember needing to pee.

He read through my lies. 'Moetie vir my liegie, Shana.'

I wanted to tell him the truth immediately. He was like my mother, my body memory tensed up. The alcohol was my saving grace – the only reason I didn't cry.

Before I could answer, Felicia stumbled drunkenly out of the front door behind me. She didn't know her father was outside. She didn't have time to react either. He reached over my shoulder and grabbed her by the face. He threw her to the ground. Pelican Heights is notorious for its loose sand – it clung to the mucous and spit and alcohol-induced sweat on her face. And he just stood there. One friend shouted, 'You can't hit her like that,' and I remember feeling she was out of line to tell a father how to handle his child. He hit her all the way home.

I went home and told my parents. My mother and a friend's mother went to speak to him the next day. We weren't allowed to sit in on the meeting, of course. It was for big people. Grootmens praatjies. I sat in the room with my friend. I watched her ice her blue, swollen face. When we got home, I asked what had happened. My mother told me that we shouldn't question what goes on in other people's homes. She had no business telling a man how to discipline his drunk, unruly daughter. 'Wat soek 'n meit soe dronk, soe laat buite?'

When I visited my friend again, the family seemed to have forgotten about the father's transgression. She was still grounded, though, because she was the child who was disobedient, a girl who had put herself in danger. Her father's actions were deemed chivalrous in comparison to her insolence.

He died many years later when I was already married. At his funeral, I stood and watched as everyone lauded him. His widow was in tears. His daughters stood there, readying their last goodbyes in their heads. Everyone spoke of what a good, stern man he was. A pillar of the community.

The pastors who had previously spoken to him about how beating his wife wasn't permissible, the community leaders who saw him beat his children. They all went just short of giving him a 21-gun salute. And he was a good man to other people: the people who didn't have to live with him or carry his heavy coffin to his grave.

A look even further back into my psyche will reveal other seemingly irrelevant happenings, that became the building blocks of my personality.

My family has a history of alcohol abuse as well as more general abuse. In the 90s, many of my mother's siblings were AA members. AA, or Alcoholics Anonymous, was something everyone in my community encouraged others to go to.

I would go as far as saying that the lower-middle class Coloured community is plagued by alcohol. But saying it isn't my place. Only learned politicians who have never lived there are allowed to speak of our statistics. I can speak of my family and the adults I was exposed to all my life, though. Women of my mother's generation had a very unique relationship with liquor. A self-respecting woman didn't drink with the men; it was a recipe for self-inflicted disaster. It was shameful, anti-feminine and certainly not Christian to be open about drinking; so I watched my mom sneak a dop or two from the geyser cupboard.

My uncles were alcoholics out loud. Before my one uncle James died, I witnessed him and his brother drink so much whiskey that they fell asleep, faces first in their respective plates of food. They burped and farted and toasted like Vikings – swollen with pride (and gout). James was also notorious for getting drunk and abusing his wife. At my sister's wedding he drank so much red wine that he started throwing wine glasses at her. His sons were livid. They wanted to attack him. But at the next family

25

function, they sat beside their father, upright and happy, as if nothing had happened. At his funeral he was also lauded as a family man – a hero.

Here, it is important to say that my mother's family lived in various parts of Mitchell's Plain. And like the different areas of the Plain, the family members each had a unique economic status. My family from Colorado were well-off, much like my aunty in Portlands. Some stayed in the painfully middle-class Westridge, and those who really felt fancy moved to Strandfontein and denounced their allegiance to the Plain in its entirety.

Another uncle, Kenny, unfortunately lived in Eastridge – the gutter of the suburbs according to my family's standards (not mine). And with life in Eastridge came alcoholism and shame. He was an officer of the law: an addict with a licensed firearm. At one point he lived with us, because his wife had wanted to leave him because of his drinking and violent ways. I was young, and the details are quite fuzzy, as I wasn't really privy to the struggles of the adults. (We don't bring up these things anymore.) Regardless, his behaviour was no secret to my extended family, who encouraged the two to remain married, because of 'the will of God', and other made-up bullshit statements that help keep wives at the mercy of narcissistic bastards.

His daughter, my cousin, was one of my closest friends when I was growing up. I remember my mom taking pity on her as the only girl in my uncle's household. He had two older sons who were the unfortunate bearers of his toxic masculinity. So, sometimes my cousin would sleep over by us. She would wear my clothes, and my mom would make sure to split all my things down the middle. But my mother also had days where she didn't want the burden of another person's child, so when her generosity was depleted, we would rip my cousin from the safe haven of our upper-class home and drive down Spine Road, to Eastridge.

She would silently cry in the back seat and I would be secretly happy she was going home because it wasn't lekker to share all of my stuff. I disliked her for being poor. It irritated me. I was told by many people that being poor was a choice.

Hulle hou mos van soe lewe. Aspris. Obviously, they liked it that way.

When we stopped outside my uncle's house he was standing in his underpants in the front yard. As we approached, I saw my mother grit her teeth in the rear-view mirror. Only in retrospect can I identify the internal struggle of her grimace. This was her goddamn problem now. This wasn't how she had planned her day. My uncle was screaming and shouting profanities to an invisible audience. He was piss drunk. His chest was pushed out, in baboon-male bravado. She drove right past the first time, parked on the next road and closed her eyes.

'Mommy, we drove past the house.' I get it, I was annoying.

Silence. She often didn't feel the need to respond to me.

'Mommy?'

'Hou jou bek, Shana,' she screamed at me to shut up.

I looked at my cousin.

'I don't wanna go home,' she mouthed.

I smiled, insincerely.

After a few minutes, my mom drove around the block and parked in front of my uncle's house.

'Kom,' she signaled my cousin. 'Bly jy inni kar,' she told me.

I sat back in the car as ordered and watched my cousin reluctantly slide off the backseat and into the street. She grabbed her smelly backpack and my mom closed the car door behind her. Her stuff always smelled like it had been wet and never allowed to fully dry. A poverty damp, the smell on all of her family's clothes.

My uncle came to the window to kiss me hello. I smelled sour whiskey on him. I didn't want to kiss him, but that wasn't an option. His puckered lips were wet.

My cousin walked into the house and didn't come back outside. My mom sped off.

'Mommy, we can't leave her here, uncle looks angry.'

I meant drunk, but saying it would have been out of line.

'Die is haar pa, Shana.' My mom was annoyed that I was being her conscience. 'Sy kannie vir iewag by os gebly het nie. Die is nou weer haar kruis.'

And that was it. She could not stay away from home, stay with us. It was her cross to bear. Your portion is your portion. I never thought to expect more than mine after that lesson.

And so, with these unwritten rules burned into my subconscious, I navigated the next 20 years of my life. Men were exempt from repercussions and women were there to be silent and enjoyed. Especially sexually, I would learn.

# Chapter 3

# A vagina monologue

My first encounter with my sexual awareness happened when I was only five years old, before it was my turn to be branded a jintoe, Jezebel, jas or any other judgemental jab by the people of my culture. This was before I had even heard of the term 'ougat', or understood the connotation the phrase 'old-fashioned' carried in the community. My kink at the time was apparently the presenter on KTV, or at least that is what I think I remember about the day I first orgasmed independently. Little did I know, independently would be the only way I would orgasm consensually until marriage. A ghastly waste of a G-spot, in my opinion.

I have an older sister. She is much older, by 13 years. This particular day my sister was home instead of at school and my mother had chosen to spend time with her, instead of bothering with my annoying five-year-old shenanigans. They made themselves comfortable in one of the rooms of our Woodlands, Mitchell's Plain home, while I was left to entertain myself in the lounge. And, oh boy, did I.

Our furniture at the time was a wooden set, with detachable cushions. They were avocado green and suede; smooth to the touch. The cushions smelled of Gunston cigarette smoke and my father's cologne, another notable marker of what attracted me sexually. I am still partial to a man who smells of blue-collar workers and smoker's breath. I took the top cushions from the settee and laid them on the floor. Stomach and G-spot down, I purposefully grinded the fabric, inhaling the smoky, manly aromas. If I close my eyes, I can still feel the corduroy-like lines of the fabric scraping against my cheek. A sudden spank on my behind both ended and elevated my experience. My mother, standing appalled, slipper in hand, was absolutely mortified at the discovery. At least, I think she was mortified. We have never discussed it again.

And this would be the recurring theme in my sexual awakening. Silence. Nothing even slightly taboo was discussed; in turn I learned nothing. I was left to my own devices when it came to puberty, sex and general interaction with the other sex.

An important thing to bear in mind is that our sexual preferences and dislikes, and the things we are attracted to, are all embedded into our psyche from as early as our toddler years. Much the same as how our sexual identity is developed around the age of three or four.

In my own experience, I knew that my vagina was important to my identity as soon I could understand words. Everything, from the moment you find out that you are a girl and that there are boys, is centred on it. From schoolgoing age, I was cognisant of the fact that my peers were starting to interact 'sexually' with each other and a lot of this interaction depended on how attractive they were. The pretty girls were favoured by the boys. This was something I knew I wasn't allowed to acknowledge, because acknowledging that I understood physical attraction, or even recognised it, would mean that I was feeling urges that were 'too old for me'. My mother would refer to my desire to touch my vagina as 'urges'. It was our code word for it and it made me feel ashamed of it. My mother wasn't doing anything wrong, necessarily, or not on purpose. Her generation had been taught that girls and women aren't supposed to enjoy anything sexual: it was perverse, unladylike. I know now that her constant shaming was her attempt at training me for the real world. But all the same, it trained my body and mind to equate sex with guilt; an effect that would stay with me through all the years of my sexual development and haunt me even into my marriage.

'Het jy weer urges gekry?' she would ask me, accusatorily, if I still had those feelings. This was usually a question reserved for bath time, when my panty was too dirty.

I would reply with an innocent, 'No Mommy, I didn't sleep today'. I equated masturbation with feeling tired afterwards. I had no idea at the time that I was first cumming and then experiencing delicious euphoria and relaxation. I think the feeling of sleepiness was the motive for my obsession.

And obsessed I was. Had I not been shamed for it, I probably would have done it all day, anywhere. I was fascinated by how, just before it felt good, I was immobilised. I had no idea what I was doing was sexual, but I knew I was supposed to hide it away. I didn't even know if other humans had discovered this trick. It felt like it was my personal superpower. Even in my teens I didn't know it was actually masturbating. Porn and crude boys were my only sources of sexual information and from what I gathered, I needed to put my fingers in my vagina to masturbate and I wasn't doing that. I was merely rubbing my thighs together and stimulating the top part of my koekie. Did that count? I wasn't going to ask.

School wasn't much help. From the beginning, sex was presented as something girls kept as a gift for boys. And if a boy was worthy, he would do things for you to get it. Transaction, but not like prostitution. The difference is unclear, like most things

31

regarding sex and women. Only boys have a recognised sex drive and from what movies, books and afterschool specials explained, they can't control it. The most that girls were told about our bodies is that we menstruate and that it was dirty. Natural and a lifegiving miracle, but dirty and not an excuse to slack.

I remember the day I got my first period. I was ten. At home, the concept of periods had been explained to me, sort of. My mother and sister were open about their time of the month and I had seen sanitary pads in their drawers and dressing tables. I didn't fully understand the correlation between periods and boys and babies, but I did know that once you started menstruating, you were a 'big girl'. I was in Grade 4, so every girl in my class was experiencing the same thing. Either they had gotten their period and walked around with their pads in little sling purses as a badge of honour, or they were waiting patiently to join the club.

I have never been brave enough to discuss this moment with a therapist. I can write about my darkest emotions and most humiliating threesomes on the internet for thousands of strangers. But looking someone in the eye while describing my innermost feelings as a young girl discovering my sexuality in my father's house feels a little bit too intimate.

That day, I felt a trickle of wetness on my panty after the usual long day of school and play. I had been at my friend's house after school and when I got home, I rushed to the bathroom to pee. I looked at my underpants, hammocked between my knees as I sat on the toilet. What I saw was neither blood, nor the usual yellow stains of shame. The goo on my panty was a brown, streaky mess. This was my first brush with sexual anxiety. My mommy was going to be so disappointed when she washed my underwear. But when I showed her, she smiled and said 'Jy is nou 'n groot meisie.' It was my initial 'welcome to the club' and soon every woman in my family was given the news that I was now a member. It felt lekker to see their faces when they heard the news. 'Mmmph, excuse me!' they jokingly mocked me for being a big girl – and I liked it.

The novelty of periods wears off pretty quickly once you get that first nasty cramp in the right ovary. Experiencing diarrhoea, horniness and flashes of irrational emotions all while having to remain a lady is maddening and, eventually, boring. But I wasn't yet tainted by this information, that in my community comes only through lived experience. This is true of most things women from my culture experience because of the way sexuality, love, marriage, periods and anything taboo is both shrouded – not talked about – and worshipped as tradition. Had I known that enduring that monthly nastiness would be one of the easier experiences I would have to adjust to as a woman, I probably would've ended my life right there. But I didn't know at the time.

And then, in 1998, my life changed as much as it could for a young Coloured girl in a very recently apartheid-free country.

When I was ten years old, my father was promoted. But the extra money wasn't what hurt me. The transition was. Nothing is more dangerous and potentially damaging than new money with old habits. With our new lavish lifestyle came new wants and needs and a very new social status. I was taken from the government school I attended with my mom who was a teacher and put into a private, previously whites-only Catholic school. We had moved from Mitchell's Plain to Pelican Heights about two years prior, but into a ghost of the home we would eventually have. Suddenly, my house went from a separate entrance with tapyt floors on a large property to a double storey with space for a swimming pool. And my friends changed from poor Coloured kids who waited for the free peanut butter bread at first break, to children from Rondebosch East who refused to admit that they were actually from Crawford.

I didn't know what the fuck was happening, but I knew I didn't belong . . . to either of the groups. But saying that of the one side was modest and saying it of the other was classist.

The strangest part of being at my new school was that I had already acquired my permanent Coloured twang and I still lived in measly old Pelican Heights. For the Mitchell's Plain kids, my double storey in Pelican Heights was impressive. Most of the kids at my new school, however, didn't even believe the area in which I had lived existed.

In the mornings, my dad would load me into his bright yellow City Council bakkie and cart me off to my new school in Plumstead. We would drive past all of my Strandfontein Primary School-going friends and bypass Zeekoevlei and Grassy Park and the other areas I knew so well and would end up in the lush, lawny aesthetic of Southfield. In the afternoon I would leave the sanctuary of extramurals and aftercare and make my way back to the sandy hills of the Heights to play with my common tjommies. And I, stuck somewhere in the middle, didn't know what accent to use, or what jokes to make, or where to put my fucking loyalty. My gham friends hated the whities and coconuts and my coconut friends were terrified of anyone across the Ottery border.

My parents didn't feel the need to facilitate my transition from government to Model C (which for the longest time I thought was pronounced Moral C). Also, at the Mitchell's Plain schools I had been revered as a prodigy. I was the teacher's child who could read better and count higher than the other kids. I was so impressive, apparently, that I went from Grade 1 straight to Grade 3.

I never did Grade 2 and sincerely believe that because of this, I skipped the developmental phase in which children learn to make authentic interpersonal connections with others ... I don't think I have ever made up the missing time.

I truly wasn't expecting to find myself at the bottom of the food chain at St Anne's Primary School. But my Colouredness really irked my new white teachers. The children there were confident and encouraged to be so – as I had been when I was the golden girl back at my Mitchell's Plain primary school. Now, because I was an intruder, the teachers met my enthusiasm with eyerolls and irritation – and my fervour for life was seen as an attitude problem. I believe that as a certain type of Coloured (darker and more accented than the Rondebosch East types my new teachers were familiar with) my presence set off red flags in the subconscious minds of those other, 'better' people. So when I acted out of line, or out of the character they were okay with me being, I was in the kak.

But for different reasons than at home. So no matter which persona I adopted, I was wrong. And for all these complicated reasons I was very, very unhappy.

One thing we didn't do in my family was show weakness. I went through these massive life changes completely silently. I didn't know any better, anyway. My understanding was that I was to be as malleable as possible. Going along mindlessly was the same as being obedient.

My new schoolmates were refined and had new toys and their parents could take them to cool places like McDonald's. They did extramurals and knew the Latin version of 'Ave Maria'. We sang 'Panis Angelicus' in a three-part harmony and had swimming as a school subject. My home friends played hocks – hopscotch – in the road. One group asked me why I spoke so funny. So I

35

copied their accent until the other group asked me why I spoke so funny. Eventually, I was so unrelatable that neither group would play with me.

How is this relevant? Well. The way the boys and girls interacted at my new school was a world apart from what I was used to and yet the same.

In my gham comfort zone I had learned the secret games like 'Alie Fondalie' and 'Rape and Moer' in crèche already. Yes, 'Rape and Moer' is the official, signed-off name of the game and it is exactly what you think it is. I am pretty sure grown-ups endorsed it and even taught us the rules – in Physical Education classes or in the streets outside our homes where we often played. For those who weren't conditioned into accepting rape culture from childhood, the game consists of two teams that compete in a soccer match with one catch: if the ball goes between your legs, consensually or otherwise, the other team is allowed to beat you up.

'Alie Fondalie' is basically just a rude recitation with sexual connotations: one of the moves involves selecting the person to go into the middle of the circle by lifting your leg and thrusting your private parts at them.

In Model C land, it was more demure; everyone was immediately classed into popular (attractive) and not popular (ugly). This was further segmented into jocks and nerds. See, the kids at private school all had TVs and could watch *Cruel Intentions* and *Clueless* further cementing their shitty demon-like personalities.

The Model C teachers were also unevolved products of less sensitive times; adults who weren't held accountable by social media social justice warriors. They could say anything to anyone, gay, black, ugly . . . everything was fair game.

At primary school, my heart was set on Dance and the Arts. This passion was approached differently by people of the late 90s.

There was nothing like the inclusive culture of the 2010s for aspiring Coloured artists in the 90s. We endured endless ridicule about how local would never actually be lekker. The B-boys and all-boy singing groups were lazy, 'lui vir regte werk'. Girls who could sing were a dime a dozen wannabes and 'Kyk vir Mariah Carey' was the kind of scathing ridicule you would endure if you even tried to sing in public. Anyone who chose the path of an artist was a spectacle by default. Unless you won something as big as the Westgate Mall singing show or were on TV, your performances were embarrassing, small fry. There was really no mercy for people who were afshowerag.

When the school decided to do an interpretation of the CS Lewis classic *The Lion, the Witch and the Wardrobe*, my nerd brain went into hyperdrive. I had an opportunity to show off in a sanctioned manner. The great thing about my school was that the biannual play was to involve everyone. This was mainly to ensure that all the parents came to the play, but it also meant that the other kids couldn't ridicule me for wanting to do theatre.

On the day that the roles were announced, each class was lined up in the assembly hall in single file and a panel of teachers sat across the front of the stage, making selections. There were no auditions for parts and by the time we got to my class, there was an obvious pattern to the choices. All the popular, petite girls got to be the White Queen's reindeer. The popular boys were soldiers and the unpopular boys were trees. All the fat dark-skinned girls like me who didn't have straight hair were chosen to be peasants. The reindeer wore leotards and Alice bands adorned with glitter and antennas. And we peasants had our teeth blacked out and wore potato sacks.

And despite the pain it caused, we accepted it because it made sense. Having the grown-ups agree that the reindeer girls were in fact the prettiest because they were light and petite was just a validation that we were getting the hierarchy right all on our own.

But it did do a number on me and because I was already sexually aware, it damaged my confidence. It also cemented my place in the primary school food chain and all the way till Standard 5 I was a bottom feeder.

I really needed clarity on the shifts I was experiencing: on the move from innocent playground shenanigans to now feeling stirrings in my loins; on my new capacity to feel embarrassed suddenly; and on why I suddenly wasn't conventionally pretty compared to lighter Coloureds, when I had been the belle of the ball with my sleek 'curly but moered' hair in Mitchell's Plain Elementary.

But I wasn't going to ask for guidance. Jas.

Saying the teachers didn't like me was just fuel for my mom to investigate what kak I was catching on to put her in the eyes.

Asking about boys would make my sister laugh, my father ashamed and my mother angry.

Let me walk you through Coloured parenting and the facade of adult authority in the late 90s to 2000s. The path of least resistance is the correct path. Children are meant to be seen and not heard.

To delve deeper, a child had no rights. Grown-ups were the authority no matter what. Age was an exemption and hierarchies the norm. Even your older siblings had control over you – they were both your authorities and your bullies. Your body was not yours – you would kiss aunties and uncles on command. If an adult gave you an instruction, you would oblige – and adults had an aversion to children who didn't jump at their command. What this meant, is that all my friends and I were trained from an early age to completely abandon our sixth sense, programming ourselves into subservience instead of independent thought. Children with independent thoughts were rude and 'uit die wil uit'. I didn't want to anger adults, because they had the right to make my life miserable. If a grown-up complained to my mother about me, I was immediately, obviously, wrong. There would be no discussion. Childhood was the 'retail' of life's phases and the adult was the customer who was always right.

I was always opinionated though, something that made my parents and teachers handle me on the offensive, not defensive, whittling my confidence down by abuse and constant reprimand. I also had a knack for observation and my superpower, still, is being able to decipher what is unspoken or underlying in conversations and other interactions. I capture the essence. I am the perpetual observer, a role that I believe makes me a storyteller by nature. Grown-ups never liked that. No one wants to look into a mirror or be deconstructed by a pesky child.

But my ability to think for myself and speak for myself and even have a sense of self was disciplined into constant submission. I was made to believe that in order to exist I needed to toe a line set by the authority that was placed above me by God. It really influenced how I navigated everything, my relationships especially. My relationship with grown-ups, my parents and sibling, and eventually, my relationships with friends and men would be shaped by this.

# Chapter 4

# . . . and women

A lesser-known fact about me, to my family at least, is that I am bisexual. Mostly gay. Yes, I am married to a man.

If I could attach a percentage to it, I would say I have always been 80 per cent for the ladies. I could go even further and say that most of the straight women I know are 80 per cent for the ladies. But I would never be so bold. Given the chance to redo my life, would I live my truth openly and risk losing my birthright, the respect of my peers and family and apparently my religion by choosing a path as sinful as homosexuality? I didn't risk it and it happened anyway.

The pain of not being able to admit who I am damaged me deeply, especially because I didn't even admit it to myself until, as a young adult, I had veered so far from my true self that I had become unrecognisable, embarrassingly stuck in the persona of a slut for men. When I didn't even enjoy them. Penis is aggressively mediocre. An inferior prize for enduring the man attached to the other end. But to keep up appearances, even when I realised I was gay, I went along with what was expected instead of what I wanted. Even more so, to be honest. I now know I was ashamed of myself – and would have rather lived in acceptable heterosexual shame than tell my mommy, my daddy and myself that I had gone askew.

Of course in the early 2000s it was anyway a little complicated for a Coloured tween from a Catholic home to announce her soft spot for pretty girls. Back then, being a moffie or tomboy was not only an insult to your family, but an insult to God. An unimaginable weight to bear for . . . You get it.

By the time I accepted my real adult lust for the women who I found appealing, I felt the need to investigate why I was so perverted. I didn't just accept it. It had to be my fault to make sense. No one I knew was openly gay, not without stereotypes and ridicule. Gay men were hairdressers, gay women were ugly and had bad haircuts. I didn't want to be ugly and have a bad haircut. There were other fears, of course, but I really didn't want a Mohawk.

And so, I delved into my own head to grasp at what could have turned me. I did everything the boys wanted me to, for fuck sakes. And the more I fucked men, the more disillusioned with them I became.

Before I disclose my discoveries and theories, I again want to clarify that this memoir isn't only about sexuality. It may seem that way, but it's because I believe I have to relay certain uncomfortable truths before anyone can truly understand my actions, and more importantly, understand the mind-set that landed me in an abusive, inescapable relationship with a sadistic narcissist.

I want to answer the antediluvian question, 'why didn't she leave?' in as thorough a manner as possible. So that people can stop asking it forever.

I am a Coloured. I am a woman.

Both of those titles have infinite interpretations. As much as this memoir is about my sexual identity as a Coloured woman and the things I have had to endure as a sexually aware person living in a very anti-sex, yet sex-driven culture, it is important to take into consideration all the other factors and seemingly unrelated experiences that merged to create my persona.

When I say that my vagina has caused most of the issues in my life, I am alluding to how being a female child of colour in the time I am from, from the place I am from, from the family I am from, has influenced every single aspect of my life. It is the reason I allowed certain people to do certain things to me. A large part of who we are is derived from who we are surrounded by.

Believe me, I am well aware that I have no qualifications to back up any broad statements about the inner workings of the subconscious mind – but I do know myself. I can say without a doubt that through the process of critically analysing my experiences, trying to pinpoint the reasons why I behave the way I do, I have identified key moments in my childhood that still affect the way I handle myself today.

As I was saying, I learned in my formative years that I had funny feelings for girls (and boys). I was well aware, however, that I was not allowed to like girls. To be fair, I was also not allowed to like boys, but it was a very different type of injunction.

I also knew pretty early on that I didn't mix well with other female children, not platonically. I assume this stems from interpersonal relationships with the women from my own family and how I was raised, as well as the many female 'friends' I made from childhood through to adolescence.

My mother was a staunch woman. She is still alive and has changed over the years, but when I was a child, the leash around my neck was very short and very limiting. She controlled everything, from the clothes I wore (well into my late teens), to the strict curfew I was given on the rare occasion that I was allowed out. I knew very little about her as a person, which I think was deliberate on her part. My opinion on 'boomers', the generation she is from, is that they didn't want children to be too familiar with them – it made them fallible. Their generation believes that familiarity breeds contempt; but I think their disconnect with the generation they birthed is perhaps the definition of what 'contempt' really is. I was raised at arm's length.

My sister, who is a very private person from the generation that is called Gen X, believes that Facebook is for sending messages, in the comment sections of unrelated posts, to keep in touch with family and friends – but never for personal affairs or insight into who you really are. The people who end posts with, 'love from Aunty Brenda and Family,' and have no social awareness, but are just slightly more hip and happening than their parents, because they were young in the 90s when people said shit like 'hip and happening'.

She was on a pedestal when I was growing up; one I created for her because she was so much older and cooler than me. Even though, because of the age gap, I didn't know her. There was the superficial 'that's my sister, I must love and respect her,' but certainly no interpersonal relationship. Not the kind that would have come from her seeing me not just as a child, but as a person. I couldn't speak freely with her, because, of course, I was a child and that would muddy the authority. This has changed in recent years and we are nursing a fresh friendship that I cherish dearly.

But on the whole, when I was a child, the women in my family (aunties, cousins and the rest of the older extended family) loved to speak of how they were 'strong women' – another 90s trend that meant they wore black lipstick and combat boots. But, looking back, I can see that the term was synonymous with being loud and rude.

And angry.

They were always so angry and reprimanding. They had a

no-nonsense, stern, 'ek is groot' vibe about them that I thought showed that they were mature. Because of them, I equated moodiness with womanhood for much longer than was necessary. They had normalised shouting at their husbands, yet remained subservient when it came to wifely duties. It was confusing to watch them slave away at cleaning and serving, while still maintaining a strict, nasty attitude that mostly served, in my opinion, to assert themselves to themselves.

At the time I thought it admirable and honestly believed that the women in my family were the ones in charge. A 'lead from the back' sort of philosophy. They always had grim looks on their faces, as if to emphasise that they weren't joking or playing around. But they had no real power when the men spoke. Their power was only over the children and they compensated by being extremely, sometimes damagingly strict mothers.

To be fair, I see now that they were the women who were thrown into the middle of a feminist revolution they didn't yet know was brewing. They couldn't be 1950s wives as their mothers had been, but they were not emotionally ready to be women of the 2000s who didn't fucking need men. Even now, many of them don't really like the new generation of career-driven, independent females who chose not to marry or have kids. But it's a dislike rooted in envy, in my opinion.

Envy and pain.

I think I adopted a hard exterior, but submitted in every relationship I ever had, because that was the lesson: subservience was fine if you looked annoyed with it. Just don't actually fight it. Even in the office environments I entered as an adult, 'bossy' women were seen as strong, though they usually toed the line and were only rude to other women and subordinates. Only very recently did I notice my own self-destructive pattern of gravitating towards bossy, obnoxious women as friends.

Whenever I encountered a woman who was bitter or overly serious, my body memory made me tense up. My mind placed them in authority, since my mother and sister were this way with me – because I was a laaitie, mos. I think my generation of Coloured girls had our wills broken so young that we took on the role of being the 'least'; in conflicts I still sometimes have to remind myself that I am no longer a child. I can only assume this is because the women who raised us were trapped in this very unique bubble. They didn't think to teach the next generation while they were surviving their own trauma and confusion. I cannot make any hard statements, though; they've never confirmed anything or apologised.

Sexually, however, I am attracted to meek women.

Damn, this is difficult.

Actually, purposefully recalling secrets is taxing. Sometimes the memories creep up on me, usually after I have been triggered by a smell, or a word, or lesbian pornography of some kind and I have to pause and resist the urge to scream in mortified nervousness. But this one I have pulled from the deepest darkest recesses of my mind, where I store all of my beatings – along with my early 2000s fashion choices. My earliest memory of sexual experimentation is of a friend I am still close to, 20 years after the fact. Even though we have remained friends into adulthood, we have never spoken of it. (For the record, I don't prefer lesbian porn because of my bisexuality; straight porn by its nature is aggressive and tailored to men. No woman wants you to punch her cunt and then come in her clean hair. Straight porn is both a testament to how little men know about what women want sexually and how little they care about what women want sexually. I find it fascinating that female, or lesbian porn needs to be called 'female porn' and porn for men is simply just 'porn'. And of course by 'fascinating', I mean absolutely not fascinating in the least. Also, boy cum is gross and tastes like brine – swallowing it is the sensory equivalent to drowning in the ocean, without the sweet, sweet release of death after.)

Regardless, when I moved to Pelican Heights, I knew no one. The area was pretty barren, as my dad was one of the first people to buy a plot of land in the mostly bushy development site. Besides our home, which was slap-bang in the centre of the area, there were three homes belonging to other families, two of whom had daughters roughly my age. Leah and Gaynor. My father introduced himself to the neighbours – much to my mother's disapproval. She didn't like to mix. An introduction seemed like an invitation to be continuously social, a sentiment I now share.

But at that stage I wasn't yet easily exhausted by company and I integrated myself into the duo, which became a kind of threesome. Over the next few years I would see these two girls often. It was a difficult thing to try to be an 'equal' friend to two girls who were already besties, so I graciously accepted the third-wheel ranking. It was a better fate than being alone in my room, especially during the excruciatingly long December holidays.

My integration into their already established bond sometimes caused conflict. Gaynor wasn't too happy about me and Leah having private jokes or spending time together alone, so things soured pretty fast – but when it came to girls, I would learn, that didn't necessarily mean that you are no longer part of the group. Frenemies and other toxic dynamics were prevalent amongst females in the playgrounds of my childhood.

I started to notice that Gaynor wouldn't open the door when I came knocking. Her mother, who was vocal about not being happy living in a developing area, would comment on me being a 'local' when Gaynor's other friends were there. Gaynor went

46

to a private school, so when these friends came for sleepovers, we weren't really invited to integrate. There were also friends from the church that both Gaynor and Leah's mom's went to and friends from the posher, more white-adjacent area they had lived in before. Even though I also went to private school, my proximity to ghamness outweighed everything.

Once I went over to play, and during the course of the morning, I saw that her mother was preparing snacks in the kitchen. At lunch time, there were three of us children, but only two snack trays.

'My mom made us a snack tray but you are spoiling everything,' she said in a thinly veiled attempt to get me to leave. She could have just said get out, because I didn't take the cue.

Unfortunately for Gaynor and her friend, I had gotten used to staying in places where people didn't want me, so I just kept playing. Her mother eventually said, 'It's time to eat. Shana, you need to go now,' and I left, without saying anything. I still wish I had turned back and said something – maybe called her a poes . . . Any punishment would have been worth it.

I went back many times, always forcing myself into the dynamic. Eventually it just fell into place: Gaynor, Leah and I would spend weekends together, playing and making up dances to Britney Spears songs. All was well in the world.

One evening, Leah came over to play and we sat in my room, talking. There was nothing strange about it, except that the atmosphere was not platonic, although I didn't know it at the time. I had no words for 'the energy changed', I just thought I was imagining it. For some reason, we started touching each other's bodies. Innocently, we ran our fingers over each other's stomachs and felt each other's skin. I remember thinking that it was wrong, but I honestly felt it was outside of my control. My

47

conscience took a back seat, commenting in my head, but not actually intervening. I can still remember avoiding eye contact with her in case she stopped, or freaked out, or ran away. I don't know. I just knew that what we were doing was natural and unacceptable at the same time. I wasn't attracted to her, I just wanted to touch her. We sat on the bed and undressed. Tops only. And she lay down on her back. I licked her navel. Then I waited for her giggling to subside, insecure about whether she wanted me to touch her more: I felt the need to read the room. I know now that my self-worth was reliant on how others perceived me. I had embodied that I was a nuisance and this translated into every aspect of my life. I licked her again, this time moving my tongue up her ribcage, onto her nipple. I could smell her body lotion and I liked it.

Leah sat up and looked at me, then stood up, put on her top and said that she had to go. It was all so sudden. I said, 'Okay,' and I walked her out the door. Even as a child I understood consent.

Back upstairs I sat on my bed and replayed everything in my head. I didn't really understand what had just happened, but I knew that I liked it and I didn't know if she did or didn't. And the more I thought about it, the more I felt ashamed.

I would have another encounter soon – but again, there would be no guidance to follow.

One day, I discovered a book in our bookshelf that piqued my interest for two reasons. Firstly, I loved reading and the title was something about questions children ask. The second intriguing element was that there was a section on how to speak to your kids about sex and an entire paragraph on 'nocturnal emissions'. I didn't fully grasp what any of the shit in the book meant, but it felt skelm to read it, so I kept going. I put it back onto the shelf and would grab it whenever I had reading time.

When I was older, my mother handed me a different book. This one had been my sister's. It was a collection of facts about the vagina. By this time, I had been through the mandatory Sex Education Week that the Grade 6 learners had to endure each year – a week that most of us had been looking forward to since Grade 4.

We knew that it was filled with taboo topics. The whole class spent that school week in the assembly hall, listening to virginal white women tell us about masturbation and pre-cum. It was a valiant attempt to scare us out of any type of sexual activity. We heard incorrect beliefs about HIV and were even warned that if we kissed too much, we could get mono. The week wasn't a laid-back, safe zone of questions and answers either. It was handled very Christianly. We didn't speak of homosexuality and if we had any questions, they were to be written on a piece of paper and answered anonymously, in discussion.

The hall was literally boarded up with blackened cardboard so that the other grades had no way of seeing what was being discussed. Some parents didn't even sign the indemnity form, so their kids had to be given alternative assignments. Imagine not wanting your child to learn about sex so much that you interrupt the fucking curriculum.

I kept my head low all week and when it came to asking questions, I opted to listen to what others wanted to know. I didn't want to ask my questions about attraction and liking girls. I was too chickenshit to even submit them anonymously.

As you can tell by the 'sex week' tradition, the school I attended was the type to pray the Angelis each day at noon and hold mass on the first Friday of each month. 'Lesbian' wasn't even a term that was used in impolite conversation. So in Grade 6 when the new girl, Caryn, entered the classroom, the tingle in my vagina

49

was a secret I knew I would have to keep forever. Especially since the last time I touched a female, she ran away. I wasn't about to risk total isolation.

When Caryn Brown entered the classroom, her androgyny caused my spirit to stir in a way that I hadn't yet felt. The other girls had shown interest in boys since Grade 5 and as much as I enjoyed hearing of their blushing cheeks and tingly tummies when Bryan Salvido and Shane Tessen changed into their swimming trunks, I hadn't experienced what they were talking about myself – not until Caryn.

I had felt compelled to lie when the other girls spoke of how the boys made them feel. I pretended that I too felt attracted to the jocks. I even pretended to smaak one boy obsessively. Not being into boys seemed freakish, the lack of attraction putting me in danger of seeming prudish and immature. If there was anything a Catholic girl wanted to seem, it wasn't prudish. What I did know, from the lessons on morality and self-worth and sexuality that I had been taught through Bible-coloured glasses, was that it wasn't natural for girls to like each other, no matter how lekker it felt. So I forced the boy thing, regardless.

Caryn was gorgeous. I still remember her in all her tomboy beauty. Tomboy was the 'polite' word we used back then to describe girls who were clearly lesbians. It was a nice way of saying 'she isn't feminine', without insinuating that there was something wrong with her sexually. It was the same way we, as a Coloured community, would refer to remedial boys as being 'good with their hands' instead of 'stupid'.

Thinly-veiled, poetically-crafted insults are the backbone of my community.

For the times we lived in, Caryn's choice of a short, faded haircut was bold. She had a girl's build, but carried herself like a boy.

She was an alpha male without the toxic masculinity. I noticed the distinction, even as a child. I didn't necessarily have the words to describe toxic masculinity – it wasn't a recognised concept – but it was definitely something I felt surrounding my world.

Her eyes were brown and her lips were flat and wide. I am not sure why I found that so attractive, but she certainly confused my 11-year-old brain. I wasn't sure how it was possible that my secret masturbation sessions were now bombarded with thoughts of a girl.

Now, when I lay on my side and squeezed the top of my koekie with my thighs, I would be thinking of a female. And it would make me cum quicker than when I forced thoughts of the boys in my class, or the celebrities on teen movies that I only enjoyed because my friends said they were funny. (I am still not a fan of the American Pie franchise, but have seen the movies almost 30 times because of an obligatory nostalgia that friends of my generation have forced upon me.) It wasn't the same as what I had experienced with Leah. This was deeper.

My first kiss with a boy was much later, in the summer holidays of 2000.

Much as I wanted my lips to connect with those of one of the popular boys, preferably in front of the entire school, my first kiss was a disappointing 'pity' affair that was the catalyst to a lifetime of disappointing heterosexual encounters.

When my aunty gave birth to my cousin in June that year, my sister and I spent some time sleeping over at her home with my cousins (her older children). My sister was there in a babysitting capacity, forging bonds with my older cousin, a bond that would carry into adulthood. The two of them would refer to each other as sisters, which I never admitted broke my heart. I was there chilling with my age-mate cousin, Louis.

51

Louis was friends with a neighbouring kid, Sherwin, and the girl who lived across the road, Zoe. Zoe was very pretty. She was light-skinned, naturally petite and had long straight brown hair that fell to her bottom. Sherwin's cousin Gareth was there for the holidays and we spent time together, playing board games and doing the things almost big kids did. I was fond of Gareth and tried to spend as much time with him as possible. He was kind, but it became glaringly obvious that his affections lay with Zoe.

Near the end of the holiday, my mom called to say that she would fetch me that Saturday. On the Friday night, we had a game of Truth or Dare – as one does, entering the adolescent years. And in an admission that broke my heart, Gareth said that he liked me as a friend. The most scathing sentence anyone can utter, especially in front of the friend who he prefers. In the next round, Sherwin chose 'dare'. I sat there, not even taking note of what was happening. My goal, to have my first kiss with Gareth, had disintegrated. I only snapped back when I heard my name on Gareth's lips.

'. . . to kiss Shana.'

I looked up. Waiting for someone to repeat what I hoped was being said.

'I dare you to kiss Shana,' he said again, for Sherwin's benefit.

Sherwin smiled and leaned over and kissed me, sticking the full length of his tongue in my mouth. How I didn't vomit is beyond me. Kissing was slimy and offensive and nothing like in the movies. He was into it, though, and when I left the next day he came to say goodbye and ask for my cell number.

I am pretty sure we dated after that, but as a residual. I just stopped responding to his SMSs at some point. Or maybe he stopped. I don't want to remember.

I was always embarrassed about the type of boy that was interested in me. I knew from the get-go that most boys were not as intellectual as I was. They said misguided but authoritative things when they spoke to me and were always so impressed with themselves for no reason. But I had been given all these silly excuses to tolerate them and 'boys will be boys'.

One day on the way to school, I was thinking about Caryn and my mom asked me what was wrong. I must have had a telling look on my face. I blurted out 'I like someone,' and she stopped the car to look at me and chat.

'Nou wie is die boy?' She was both stern and trying to do that pseudo-cool, 'hello fellow kids' cringey shit adults do to seem relatable as she asked me who he was.

But it was too late for that, I was already perpetually scared of her and the niceness was clearly a trap. She had this laugh waiting to barrel out from beneath her facial expression. I could see it just waiting there.

'Kom!' She motioned for me to spill.

It wasn't really a choice, she would soon forget the facade of a safe space and threaten me. I needed a lie. I couldn't say I liked a girl, I would be shamed and humiliated in front of everyone we knew.

'Moet ek skool toe kom en vra wat aangan?'

I could not handle the thought of her going to the school and asking about him.

'Matthew,' I said, because he was the only boy from my class she knew by name. He was a ginger and she had noticed him at parent evenings.

She laughed, rolling her eyes. I was relieved that my crush wasn't taken seriously by a grown-up. The lie would be easy to go with if there were no consequences.

'En nou? Wat, is jy geworried?' It wasn't over. I had to think on my feet. What could be bothering me that was okay to say openly?

'I just wanna know if I must tell him.' The tears started to fall down my face.

My mom's eyes widened, probably at how silly it all was. She looked the other way, out the window. I really wanted a hug, but it would have been weird to say so. Most of my requests for hugs for my mom or sister were met with 'En nou, wat gan met jou aan?' So I only hugged my daddy; he didn't mind.

'Jy sê niks vir hom nie – say nothing to him!' We were back to speaking.

She started the car. It looked like she had pulled herself back into authoritarian mode on purpose. She couldn't allow this sort of fraternising with me, it may have blurred the lines of respect we were supposed to observe.

'En jy issie by die skool vir boys nie.' She kept her face stern, but I could still see the smile. I was embarrassed and made a note to never bring up anything of that nature with grownups again.

But from here, I kept up the pretence.

Growing up without a layered mother–daughter dynamic was, I think now, the equivalent of building your dream home with sticks. My only role, as a child born into a family who already had one, was to exist. I was already an inconvenience for coming 13 years late; the least I could do was be accommodating.

The thing is, I wasn't necessarily neglected. I was fed and schooled and spoiled with material goods. But when it came to making choices, or being asked what I thought, I learned very quickly that everyone was happier when I shut up and just did what I was told.

Most offences were punishable by hidings, but offences weren't necessarily offences in the general sense of the word. When I said I didn't like something, my mother and father would say I only cared about being different, invalidating my opinion. This was the attitude they took to any ideas I might have about what I wanted to eat and what I wanted to wear . . . and in the end, I just allowed them to choose so that I wasn't in trouble. This meant that my sense of style didn't develop, but deeper than that, my sense of self didn't either. I really think it was more convenient to take my voice away and not have to deal with me than to acknowledge that I had feelings and ideas and needed to be allowed to develop them.

And my mother made it very clear early on that unless I was a carbon copy of the perfect daughter she had already raised, I really wasn't worth the trouble. My sister was a hard act to follow – an A student, who had landed a job at a seriously popular company, acing their training programmes and, in her early twenties, became the first woman in Africa to do her job.

When I was twelve, she was in her twenties and had moved out of our parental home, trying to make a life for herself. The day she left, I remember her packing her things into her white Ford Laser and hugging my father goodbye, indefinitely.

Looking back, I realise that my sister and her friends all equated whiteness with success. They all matriculated from Mitchell's Plain schools, then moved as far from Coloured people as possible. Her accent was crisper than mine and my parents'. She introduced us to sushi and the concept of joining a gym. She even owned the first cellphone I ever saw. It was a large Nokia and had a 083 number. Hella Old School. She met white friends and she and my older cousins all scoffed at anything Coloured. Suddenly, the more successful she became, the more ridiculous and cheap everything around me felt.

Even her music was superior to the drivel my friends' older siblings listened to. They weren't as refined as my sister. While they blasted Garth Taylor and Bump 5, my sister and her group of non-racial aristocrat friends swayed to Alanis Morrisette and The Cranberries. I still have 'Daffodils' and 'Linger' lyrics embedded in my brain from her 1998 breakup with her long-term boyfriend.

Our age gap was a major part of our inability to connect. At the time, the only way she knew to relate to me was her being an authority and me a child.

Of course, to me, she was so sophisticated and unattainable – everything I aspired to be as a grown-up. She was the epitome of cool, a New Age 90s chick with a great job, great hair, her own car. I desperately wanted to be her friend. Whenever she left, I would imagine her asking me to go with her. I thought up all sorts of scenarios in which we were friends. In some of these brain skits I would do something kwaai and imagine her telling me how amazing I was. It didn't matter what the scenario was, I just wanted to lay there and bask in the feeling of her being nice to me.

I even moved into her room in an attempt to be close to her. She had left most of her things in the cupboards and on the dressing table (I assume to make a swift exit). When I was alone, I would try them on and model them in the mirror.

For many years I thought she was selfish to leave me, but looking back I realise she was also still a child, just doing what was right for her mental health and her wellbeing. Perhaps the best choice to make.

But I think when I looked at the relationships my friends had with their moms and older sisters, my loss was amplified and I felt it as a void I had to fill. It's as if I longed to be able to connect with the girls that I desired in the way they connected with other girls as friends. It would explain why lines of desire and friendship became blurred for me and why I didn't establish boundaries in subsequent friendships.

Eventually, I engaged in two pseudo-homosexual relationships as an adult – one at college and one when I had already had my son. Both of these women were my 'best friends' at the time, but there was always an unwritten ownership we felt towards each other that we wouldn't have been comfortable to admit out loud. They have both since come out as queer and I cheer them on from outside their lives. One of them is a musician. One is a teacher. I like that they're living their truths now.

As for me, even as a grown-up in my early 20s, I chose to hide myself and my identity because I couldn't connect with women on any level. Being awkward already as a friend and revealing I was attracted to women too, was too messy a situation for me. The thought of rejection from a woman in any capacity was an open wound. So, I only went for men. It was both easy because I wasn't fully repulsed by men and could swing both ways ... and difficult because every relationship I had ever been in, even friendships, was more of a performance than an actual, authentic connection.

# Chapter 5

## Where the boys are

At school, I learned very quickly that my top-heavy physique wasn't desirable to the adolescent eye. When I say 'top-heavy', I don't mean big tits; I mean big shoulders. I can only think of Gru from *Despicable Me* as a pop culture reference.

Going through high school in the early 2000s as a conventionally unattractive Coloured girl who had curly hair and disproportionate curves was like going to war. I would have much rather been shot with a rifle at close range. Before, my insecurities had mostly stemmed from pop culture and a bad relationship with my mother and sister, but they would now manifest as wanting to be liked by the real-life teenage boys and girls that surrounded me every day for the next five years. And pop culture. Disgustingly unevolved, Paris Hilton and Nicole Richie dominated, go-on-a-diet, Von Dutch pop culture. The social climate's switch from Spice Girls to *Mean Girls* was anything but a smooth transition for girls who looked like me. My WWE aesthetic seemed to be an affront; it angered boys for some reason – at least the boys my age. Older men seemed to like me; and always commented on how lekker I would be when I turned 18. It was all that kept me going, honestly.

There were two acceptable standards of beauty when I was a teenager – and they were very similar to the 90s, just less apologetic. Everything was fierce and direct. Think Simon Cowell, *Cruel Intentions, Clueless.* Either you were an actual white person with straight hair, a thin, toned body and green eyes; or if you were a woman of colour, you were as light-skinned as possible, with straightened hair and a thin body (usually achieved by a strict diet of dried fruit and entjies).

The boys quickly made it clear that I wasn't desirable. And teenage boys, at least back then, weren't well versed in either tact or empathy. By Grade 9 I was trying to conform as much as my genetics would allow and I had cut my long, thick hair into a bob (See: Hairstyle reserved for five-year-old white girls) so that I could manage it myself. Managing my hair meant blow-drying it on the highest heat, then ironing it down and swirling it in the ass part of a pair of stockings, in both directions, through the night, to achieve a pin straight, 'natural look' in the morning. I mostly achieved an indiscreet indent across my forehead, punished by in-the-know Coloured boys laughing in my face at my futile attempt at beauty. At the same time, wearing my natural hair (which was a curly mess that grew upwards instead of down) was seen as insolence. My mother, Coloured girl 'friends' with 'worse' hair than I and the school would deem it untidy and disrespectful to the institution I attended. My hair was against the code of conduct, which I can tell you, didn't make me feel too lekker about my God-given aesthetic. I only found out years later that wearing my hair 'wild' was a political statement. That particular can of worms warrants a memoir on its own, though.

Regardless, not looking the part of what was considered beautiful meant that I wasn't eligible to play hard to get.

By Grade 9, I had only been kissed once and I had thrown the idea of lesbianism out the window. Now, my quest was to earn a kiss from one of the popular boys, to validate some part of myself that I can't quite pinpoint anymore.

For context, in my year it seemed that the highest honour for a girl, besides 'not being like other girls' was being 'bevoeled' by the popular boys. The popular girls were always caught up in rumours of being fingered at the back of the school bus. They wore these rumours with both outward shame and internal pride at being desired. I so much wanted to be a part of it.

When Bradley came to our school in Grade 9, I immediately deemed him out of my league. A spiky-haired, troubled youth, he was everything I knew I wanted to hide from my mommy. He clicked with the cool crowd: the girls with the actually straight bobs and the boys who played rugby. But he noticed me. Or perhaps he noticed my desperation. Either way, he gave me his attention and, although I wasn't quite sure why he spoke to me, I was willing to do anything not to lose it. In the afternoons, a group of us (Bradley included) used to walk to the house of a classmate and smoke cigarettes. Tamara's mom was pretty cool with us hanging out at the house and she was allowed boys in her room. Obviously, Tamara was white. One day in a game of Truth or Dare, Bradley leaned in to blow smoke into my mouth. I thought he was gonna kiss me and I stuck my tongue into his mouth . . . for the longest five seconds of my life, he didn't reciprocate . . . Then, he quickly licked my mouth . . . and pushed me away. I realised what had just happened and pretended I didn't notice. Everyone else had noticed and a silence befell the room that I can't adequately capture with words.

I wasn't deterred, though.

Mortified, yes. Deterred . . . No.

For the next few months, the more he ignored my advances, the more I asked my friends to talk to him about me.

'Make reg, man?' The phrase, a crude way of asking someone to be your wingman, was a vocabulary staple of Grade 9 Shana.

I know, this is painful to read (probably not as painful as it is to write . . .) but at the time, I was oblivious to how he couldn't be into me if I was 100 per cent compliant. I mean, compliance had earned me favour at home and had gotten me a few friends to sit with at school in the afternoons . . . surely having someone around who was willing to oblige him in every way was desirable? That there isn't a true crime documentary about me on Netflix is testament to how my strict parents didn't allow me out after dark.

One Friday midyear, Bradley and I ended up in the same detention room.

I was ecstatic. I can still remember the schoolgirl euphoria that encompassed me. I had never felt anything so intensely and wouldn't soon again. My vagina actually felt tingly. He sat down next to me.

The next few minutes aren't clear, but I know I ended up handing him a piece of paper: 'Will you go out with me?' I saw him stare at the request for the second longest five seconds of my life. He started to write his reply . . . And immediately, I was filled with regret. There was no way out of this now.

'YES.'

He said yes. I smiled for the duration of detention.

I found it weird that he didn't look back and smile at me. He didn't react, really. Only years after the fact, I realised that he didn't even talk to me for the rest of the detention period. I know that subconsciously I noticed a lack of excitement in both his reaction and in my gut. I knew this wasn't how the moment should have played out, but I was willing to accept it nonetheless. Perhaps he just wasn't big on emotion. My mom wasn't. My family wasn't. That didn't mean they didn't love me. Boys also weren't very caring by nature. He was obviously shy. I would make him smaak me. I'd just allow him to touch me – that was the plan. My 13-year-old thoughts were embarrassingly common. When detention ended, he disappeared. I expected him to at least want to wait for me . . . shouldn't we vry or something?

Still, I went home ecstatic. He had said yes.

Now, I didn't grow up in the time of social media, or chat applications, so not hearing from him wasn't too strange. On Saturday I phoned his house. A few kids from school were there. He couldn't really talk. He seemed distracted.

'Aweh, Shana,' he said on Monday at school.

That was enough to make me blush. He had approached me while I was walking through the quad, on my way to sit on the bleachers near the cool kids so they could see me acting cool and perhaps change their minds about me. 'Hello Bradley,' I giggled.

'We mos jolling?' He winked at his friend, who I only now realise was stifling a laugh.

I smiled, but the tone of the sentence upset me. 'Jolling' wasn't as serious as going out. I felt demoted, but was willing to take what I could get. Even the fact that people saw him talking to me. He made small talk and put his arm around me, winking enough times for me to be completely submissive. When the bell rang, I expected a kiss on the cheek, or something I could brag about.

Instead, I received a simple 'You always got money, neh? You Pelican Heights kinnes are rich . . .'

I didn't know how to respond, although I felt a little proud that he saw me as a rich girl.

'Don't you wanna buy me a five rand Gatsby piece?'

The rest of the week was similar. I didn't see him at school on Friday, but I ended up in detention again. Detention was quiet. A mutual girl-friend of Bradley and I sat next to me. The conversation didn't take long to turn to him.

'I didn't see Bradley today,' I told her.

She looked smug and proud. 'They actually all bunked at the vlei today. You must hear the stuff that happened.'

'What happened?' I asked.

She opened her mouth in excitement. Then she paused, 'Naai, I can't tell you. Our activities is only for the group to know, you wys?' She made everything sound so cool and exclusive.

But against my better judgement, I blurted: 'We going out.'

Silence.

'Who is going out?' She was truly confused. And verbatim is the conversation that followed:

'Me and Bradley. Since last week Friday.'

'Don't talk kak . . .' [*Laughs in popular kid style.*]

'Why you say I am talking kak?'

'He was then getting bymekaar with whatshername.'

Silence.

'When did he ask you out?'

'I asked him.'

In her defence, her expression went from ridicule to sincere pity for me. She hugged me. But like I was an abandoned puppy.

'Shana, he's a playa, man. You not the type of girl brasse go for in high school. You more for when they settle down.' I am still not fully sure what that means.

The rest of that conversation is a blur, but I know I called him that night, on his house phone and he said among other things that 'I said yes because I didn't want you to feel kak'. I felt numb, mostly. I don't think that I allowed myself to fully understand what he had done, or how silly I must have looked. By this point in my life, feeling nothing was a default and when I saw him again, I would encounter my very first brush with sexual assault and feel almost nothing. Almost.

He invited me over to his house. He wasn't in school much that week, but said a few friends would be at his place while his mother was at work. I was over the moon. I wanted all the kids from his school crew to see me at his place, hanging out.

The only variable was whether my mother would allow me to go. Instead of being honest, which to be fair was unheard of for kids from Coloured homes, I asked my mom if I could sleep at my cousin's house in Strandfontein. The plan was flawless. This was a cousin on my father's side of the family, so the rules were naturally less strict in her home. On that Saturday morning, my cousin and I walked to Bradley's home. We were greeted by him and two guys. Neither of them was from school.

Inside, there were other guys smoking dagga from pipes, which I hadn't seen up close before. When they were done smoking, they opened beers and sat on the couches in his mother's lounge, rubbing their odours into the innocent fabric.

'Wil jy drink?' the ugliest one asked me. His confidence made him as intimidating as the other, more attractive guys. I pretended that I was eager to drink their beer, even though I had only had alcohol a handful of times before. But Bradley seemed to be a pro at staying upright while intoxicated. And I am not talking about his spine. When things quietened down, after everyone's dop was trekking, he asked me to sit with him in his room.

'My brasse will look after your cousin.' He laughed so sincerely that I didn't feel threatened in any way. In my head, he meant that they would entertain her while he tried to cajole me into touching his impressive penis. I thought that I was supposed to think it was impressive because of its large silhouette on the side of his PT shorts. I really didn't know what a penis was supposed to offer. We got to his room and sat down on a slightly

64

lopsided double mattress. I can still remember a deep divot in the bottom half, where I assume his feet would go if he lay down on it the proper way.

He kissed me, which I expected, but when I noticed that two of his friends were watching us through the glass panel above his door, he pushed me down and shoved three fingers into my vagina.

I didn't like it. But I didn't want it to look like I didn't like it.

The friends stormed in.

But not to help me.

They laughed.

They all smelled his fingers.

I didn't want to make a scene. He put his arm around me, assured me he was just joking and accompanied me to where my cousin was. She was no longer in the lounge, but in a different bedroom. His mom's, I assume. She was with one of the other guys. The state I found her in isn't my story to tell.

He reminded me in front of everyone that I was wet. So, how could he have forced me? My mind couldn't fully comprehend that I had been violated, though. I mean, he was my friend and he went to the same school and knew the same people. He wouldn't do anything to me that wasn't fine. Normal kids probably behaved this way. I was more concerned that my cousin didn't make a scene or jeopardise my friendship with him by going overboard and being angry or rude to the boys. She didn't. We laughed it off, sort of. I actually don't know what we did, but the guys smoked again while she and I sat there and then walked us halfway to her house as a courtesy.

He kissed me goodbye.

I went to bed that night with butterflies.

And a lot of confusion.

65

All I remember is that when Monday arrived, Bradley had been expelled. The group he was always with had done drugs on the previous trip to the vlei and a Muizenberg resident had spotted them and called the school.

Later that year, during the school holidays, there was a knock at my door.

My mom is a teacher and was in a holiday workshop and my dad wasn't yet medically boarded at this point, so I was alone at home most days. Bradley had walked from Strandfontein to see me. I was elated. I was flattered. Less so when I saw eight of his friends further up the road, making their way towards my home. Two boys from the day with my cousin were there.

Now when I say 'Bradley's friends', think of all the boys you know, who prefer to be called by their street names. Ike, Pung, Miagi, Juvi, Koppe, Boere, Miley. All in BadBoy sweaters, buff platforms and early 2000-era spikes. The extra-long kind of spikes that require glycerine soap and excellent posture to maintain. When I let Bradley in, all of them walked through the door and bolted straight for my room. I am not sure how they knew where it was, exactly. Bradley stayed behind and once they were all inside, he kissed me. His mouth was so dry.

'We in the area here by another kin. So I mos remembered, you mos live here.'

I was very impressed that he remembered. We lammed and vryed for a while and I completely forgot that his friends were in my room. I told him I missed him at school. He told me he needed to borrow my phone.

'Why do you need my phone?'

'I wanna show my mom. This is the one I want for my birthday. Don't be so. We mos know each other long.' I was sceptical, but not enough to assert myself.

66

'Promise you will bring it back?'

'Yes, I will be back in an hour. I will come alone.'

You can't make this shit up.

'... But don't let this brasse see you giving it to me. They skelm.'

My mind honestly believed that he was looking out for me, by making me aware.

'We must first go buy tik when we go now. For that kin mos.'

My eyes widened.

'You also want?' he asked me.

I didn't. But I didn't reply.

'Okay now I wys you what, I'ma take this phone with to the merchant to tell him I'm gonna sell it for the money. Then when he give the tik, I will bring it back. I'll get money again to pay him man. He is my bra. He must just see I have the phone.'

I knew that absolutely none of that was logical. But I chose to believe that I was the one that didn't understand how the 'cool people' operated.

I was silent, but didn't want to be the uncool and say no to drugs.

'Then we lam, just me and you in your room?'

He left around 2pm.

I called his phone at 3pm.

I called his phone at 4pm.

I called his phone at 5pm.

I called my phone. It was off.

My parents got home at 6pm.

And they wanted to know why I hadn't answered my phone.

'Ek phone vir jou al heel dag, Shana. Wie was hier?'

The kaare started to swirl around my head.

'A boy from school came to visit. He stole my phone.'

My mother, livid that I had let a boy in the house, put me in the car and drove me to Bradley's home.

'Jy kry nou daai phone van daai klong af.' She waited in the car, 'Ek ken mos vir Bradey, Clynn se vriend. Ek het vir jou gesê jy moet weg bly van sukke mans.'

If she hadn't told me to stay away from boys like Bradley before, she definitely had now. I walked up to his well barricaded home and rang the bell.

I rang it several times.

I started shouting that if he didn't come out, I would call the police.

Then, when he opened the door, he slowly walked up to the burglar bars and asked me to kindly keep my voice down.

'The phone is gone Shana. We tik'd it out. Please don't shout, you gonna wake my mommy.'

'Bradley, you stole my phone.'

'Jas, you gave it to me.'

I left, defeated. I don't know why I didn't call the cops. Maybe I feared it would make Bradley think I was uncool.

In Grade 10, after Bradley's exit, Shannon was my first actual boyfriend. I had never been anyone's 'love' interest before. I was 14 when we started dating. He was also attending Muizenberg High. It was the early 2000s and as I mentioned, everyone was living in an American teen movie. There was no empathy for nerds and poor kids. The cool kids were clad in Von Dutch, Diesel and toted Motorola Razrs. The uncool kids sat in the quad, avoided the field and took Jazz.

The music teacher, Mr Kruit, had had his eye on Shannon since Grade 8. Shannon played the bass guitar and didn't mix with the common kids. He spent break times learning riffs with Kruit and laughing at obscure pop culture references he had no business understanding. Shannon was half Coloured, half Indian. He came via the Muizenberg junior school and had a stellar behaviour record.

I on the other hand was loud and outspoken. The teachers knew me for being straightforward, a trait less admired at the time, especially in girls with my particular flavour and background.

I didn't know that they had interpreted my flair and charisma as aggressive. Loud was how my family operated, mos. I was a child, after all. But I now know that when you're a Coloured child that is Coloured outside of the lines, you're halfway to guilty. Just like at primary school, my confidence was obnoxious and my honesty was disrespectful.

Also, after being at the bottom of the food chain at St Anne's Primary, I was relentless in pursuit and torture of nerds. So I didn't join the music crew immediately. I even pretended I hated Drama. From Grade 8 to 10 I was the loud, obnoxious, gham girl who didn't do very well. I didn't do sports. I told jokes during lessons. I was on the VIP list for Saturday detentions. Shannon and most of my friends were nothing like me.

When Grade 10 came around, I had an epiphany that taught me I was heading for disaster. My best friend at the time, who was always top of the grade, had been warned by teachers and her parents that hanging with someone like me would only bring her down. We had been given the 'you guys are in the senior phase now' talk, and the people who would be prefects had already been pre-selected for grooming. We were split into the winners and losers of the future.

My friend sat in the quad with me one day, crying.

'My mom spoke some sense into me, Shana,' I can only remember snippets of our convo.

'You listened to your mommy about not being my friend?' I

69

wanted to ridicule how ludicrous and uncool her admission was. I couldn't relate to the mentor-type bond she obviously shared with her mother.

'Yes, she gave me perspective.'

'Okay.'

'If I want to be the head girl, I can't be friends with you.' She was visibly distressed. And weak. 'Not the way you're going.' Apparently her trajectory excluded my tragic story.

'What do you mean?' I had never seen myself as a loser. Sure, I knew people didn't like that I spoke my mind, but I had never been allowed to keep my thoughts to myself, to have secrets before. I didn't respect myself enough to guard my words, not even for self-preservation.

When I joined the class in Grade 10 and Mr Kruits' golden boy started to like me a little bit more than his instrument, I was no longer a child in a school – I was the enemy.

I wasn't very good-looking, though. My father's genes are strong and our dik lippe and fast foreheads need an incubation period, which happens to be puberty. I grew into my lips after matric. So when I had the chance to have an actual fucking boyfriend, it didn't matter that he was an overweight, uncool band geek.

I liked that someone liked me. And it was as innocent as high school romances would go. But he had one trait that made me absolutely cringe.

He had a white accent.

I didn't know that I didn't like Coloured boys who didn't sound Coloured. But I liked him. He didn't treat me like other boys did. He said I was beautiful. He even gave me my first Valentine's Day present. He dropped it at my house. My family liked him too. My mom even allowed him to visit me.

70

I feel it is important to note that I know that my stories seem conflicted, especially the way that people in my life responded to Coloured accents, Coloured beliefs and so on. But, looking back, society took strange leaps at strange times. What was acceptable, what was made fun of, all depended on which set I was with and when I was with them.

My nuclear family fell slap-bang in the middle. This was the same for my Pelican Heights and Muizenberg High School friends. We were not quite gham, not quite sturvy Coloureds who didn't like gham or sturvy Coloureds. So, while we sort of embodied the same traits as the people we ridiculed and deemed 'phony', we were not self-aware enough to see the irony or hypocrisy. It is a very convoluted thing to explain to an outsider.

So in the instance of Shannon – even though a Coloured accent was devalued at the time – introducing him to my family was embarrassing, because he sounded like a whitey. He didn't fit into the sweet spot we thought we occupied in the middle.

My mom's family received him well, though. They found his accent endearing, but his proximity to white people made him less cool, in some ways. Coloured ouens were expected to have a certain swagger. A -ness between gangster and professional that women loved and employers hated.

Shannon had none of this. He had a goofy laugh and made jokes about Slipknot and early gaming references that were too obscure for my crowd. Still, he smaaked me and I honestly smaaked him.

He was also very anti-gham, which both kind of opened my perception and made me recognise certain undertones of ghamness that I had never noticed before. One civvies day, for example, I wore a very trendy All Star boxer boot and a pink sweater, in line with what every other Coloured girl coveted in 2004. He and his white friend looked at me and giggled.

71

'You so gham!' It was the first time that sentence was directed at me.

'What do you mean? This is fashion.' I was defensive and a little hurt.

'Fashion for gham,' he said.

He wasn't being vindictive, but it stung. It also sparked an idea for me. I realised that different social groups had different ideas of what was stylish. Years later the memory hit me when I watched an episode of *Ugly Betty*, in which her Latina community 'beautified her'. Betty went to her office (a white corporate space) decked out in the hoop earrings of her people and as soon as she stepped in, felt like a pinata instead of a fashion writer.

And so, I started to believe that even when white style was wrong, it was right.

Shannon and I dated fairly briefly before I met his mother. She was younger than the other moms in the grade. I noticed that immediately. She was a petite, Coloured lady with a short I-mean-business haircut. The music class had been invited to sing at the Seaforth Restaurant that Mr Kruit frequently got shitfaced at, as a way for the jazz band and singers to get comfy as a crowd. Our parents were invited and the night was fun for the most part. After supper, I sat alone at the table putting on lip gloss, when I felt a hand on my shoulder.

'What size bra do you wear?'

I looked up and giggled. It was an odd question to ask, but the fact that it was a woman asking made it even more uncomfortable.

'Sorry, I am Shannon's mom. What size bra do you wear?'

'Okay, I am Shana. I wear a 32 C.'

'Oh. Are you Shana? Okay. I'll get your number from Shannon.'

She worked for a large fashion label and introduced herself

72

under the guise of wanting to offer me modelling work. Of course, she was sussing me out.

He invited me over to his house a few weeks later. When I arrived, his mom was in the lounge and his grandmother was in her room. They both made an effort to look at me. Like really fucking look at me. I remember being greeted, but no one smiled. It was my first encounter with the mother–son pseudo-romantic relationship that I think comes from women having to encounter every flavour of shitty man, then falling in love with the men they give birth to, because the idea of moulding a man from scratch is enticing. Unfortunately, this usually creates incompetent, entitled mommie's boys who expect unconditional love while they eternally behave like 12-year-olds. And when they get married, or find girlfriends, these moms feel cheated – and take it out on someone's innocent daughter.

Some weeks later he visited me. My parents had gone to the shop, just for an hour or so. Shannon's mom dropped him and asked to see my parents. I explained that they would be there shortly. She left and arrived back ten minutes later. She was frantic. She left again and came back again in ten minutes. It was causing her an actual panic attack. I had never seen a grown woman display such visible emotion. It was unsettling and embarrassing. Shannon was embarrassed too and kept apologising to me.

It's important to say that he and I were not alone in my home. Some of my girlfriends were there and we were sitting outside. But still, she was convinced that I was trying to molest her son, or that we were going to perform public, underage coitus. When she turned up the seventh time I told him it might be better if he left. I chalked it up to his mom being a psycho and not really about me as a person.

73

Then, that following week, I was summoned to the school's counsellor.

The counsellor was a pasty white lady, who didn't have a very welcoming face. She was a strange one. She always had the popular girls in her office. It seemed like she was their friend instead of one of the staff; like Buffy the Vampire Slayer and her friends always hanging with Giles the librarian. From the moment I walked into her office, it was obvious that she knew who I was and that she wasn't impressed with me.

'Hi Shana, sit down.' She didn't seem to think I needed easing into an awkward situation. I had no idea why I was there. I did what I was told though. And sat on the chair furthest from the door.

Then Shannon's mom entered. And then Mr Kruit.

'You're dating Shannon, right?' Pasty asked me. I had no friends in this circle.

'Yes, I am.' I looked at his mom.

'I don't want this type of girl with my son.' There were no holds barred.

'She's made his marks go down in music,' Mr Kruit tromboned.

'I called the school before, to keep them separated. I don't want him in her class. I don't recognise my son anymore.'

'Sharna,' Pasty didn't care to learn my name. 'You aren't to go near Shannon anymore, his mom is really unhappy.'

As a child, I didn't think to lay a case. I fully understood that, because of my calibre, I would hamper Shannon's life. It wasn't the first time my calibre had been mentioned and I agreed with them. Being convinced that I was 'less than' as a child had made it easier for me to step aside so that everyone around me shined.

It seems insignificant, but this particular incident affected the way I chose men from this point on. I never again pursued anyone who seemed above me. I was always scared that I would again sit through an intervention to be reminded of my place.

Shannon didn't leave me though and pursued me anyway. I liked that he went against his mother. A few months later Mr Kruit caught me sitting on Shannon's lap during an afterschool rehearsal and shouted at me so loudly that I had a panic attack.

He said I was a whore who had destroyed his star pupil.

That my type of Coloured girl was poisonous.

I reported him to the deputy principal, Mr Finch, who told him to apologise to me. And that was all. He called me out of class and took me for a walk around the field.

'I shouldn't have said that to you, Shana. You're still a child.'

I said, 'It's okay, I forgive you.'

What else was I supposed to say? I was a child. He was a grown man. Grown men have a hall pass. The rules of the world I was from. That is all I knew.

I can take you back even further.

The first time I was sexualised by a grown man I was only 11 years old. Before I had even met anyone from my high school.

I had been victim to the odd inappropriate observation by men before, but the first time I really felt that a man was sexually attracted to me was in Standard 5, when my cousin Laura's boyfriend, Garth, made a point of giving me his attention. He was around 20 years old. He was tall and smelled of expensive cologne.

I've explained that my family works on an age hierarchy. Because he was dating my older cousin, he was an authority. It was exciting when he spoke to me like an equal though. He made me feel like a big girl.

Family functions were commonplace at the time. My maternal grandmother was still alive, so the family had a reason to meet up back then. Though I was one of the younger cousins, so I was excluded from most of the conversations.

Standing with my older cousins was a surefire way to get my sister to ask me publicly if I thought I was grown up. The paradox of being a young Coloured girl is that you are shamed for being wet behind the ears, then punished for wanting to be mature. Ougat, mos. Damned if you do, a laaitie if you don't.

Garth would always find a way to converse with me. He would sit with me on the outskirts of the socialising. There was the slightest sense of doing something wrong. I felt the attraction. But he made it clear as I got older that pinpointing what we were doing would kill it. It would be childish. I didn't want to upset him, or spoil something so exhilarating.

I always looked forward to visiting my cousin's house.

Whenever he kissed me hello or bye, his lips were parted ever so slightly. But he never did anything more than insinuate. He didn't touch me.

Conversations would turn to hypothetical sexual scenarios and comments on my beauty. He made a point to say that my youth was an attribute.

My innocence was currency. I wasn't uitgerek like my older cousins. 'Fresh meat,' he once said and I blushed.

Then, one day I arrived at a family event and he greeted me, but didn't come to sit with me. Instead, he sat with my other older cousin, Jade. The whole afternoon. He didn't kiss me hello or goodbye. He didn't react to our inside jokes or give me a knowing nod when I snuck off to smoke.

I watched them. It burned my chest the way she laughed at his jokes.

To make a common story short, I didn't see him at family functions for a while – nor Jade – because he and Jade had cheated on Laura. Laura found out and had a conniption, punching Jade in the face. The family divided into Team Laura and Team Jade. Team Jade was victorious and Jade and Garth married soon after. There were no repercussions for Garth. He was welcomed back into the family's good graces with open legs. Or arms. Or hearts. Basically everything was opened besides our minds.

This is both here and there.

It is notable that my father despised Garth and said daily that he was a vullis. My father has a vullis-o-metre second to none. On the night of my sister's wedding, Garth was there with his pregnant Jade, who was tired from just being fucking pregnant, probably. My dad hosted an afterparty, but when Jade said she was too tired to party, Garth insisted that he would still be going and she could go home and sleep. My dad said very loudly in front of everyone, 'Gan huis toe met jou vrou – go home with your wife.' A sentiment I detested him for. But looking back, he was the smartest one in the room.

When I matriculated, I was 17 years old. Garth was in his twenties and even though he was married into my family, our flirting had continued.

While awaiting the release of my matric results, I received an SMS.

'Hey sexy, did you pass?' I showed my friend Felicia. She had slept over the night before so that we could get our results together. Those December holidays had moved so slowly towards results day. We couldn't bear another second of anticipation. His message was a delicious distraction.

I 'back and forthed' with him in flirty texts. I knew I was doing something wrong, but my cousin meant nothing to my thin, young self. It was her own fault for not captivating the man she stole. He treated her badly, but I always wondered what she did to 'provoke' him. He was always nice to me.

77

'I cannot wait till you're 18 so that I can fuck you.' The message gave me butterflies. It validated what I had assumed for the last six years. He did in fact see me as a grown woman.

If he hadn't been caught fucking someone else before my 18th birthday, getting divorced from Jade soon after, I would have probably thrown him some teenage pussy.

What I didn't know was that my youth wouldn't last forever.

# Chapter 6

# The boy who broke my brain

At this point in my life, my disregard for other women and their emotional bullshit was a high I loved riding. When I entered college, I felt on top of the world. I was newly single: I had dumped Shannon to pursue better sexual options and I was finally 'big', meaning I wasn't a school laaitie anymore. I had made it into the majors.

I had sort of come into my own near the end of high school. I only realised afterwards I was just in the 'we are Matrics of the school, we all family now' bubble. Humans tend to do that pseudo-family roleplay in almost every social setting – and I was deep into it. Pride for being the oldest – it meant sweet fokkol, but we all like feeling important. I was the school's lead actress in the plays, too. And a jazz singer in Mr Kruit's band. Everyone knew my name.

I hadn't expected to be surrounded by gorgeous blondes and chiselled white boys, all the belles of the ball of their respective school drama clubs, when I set foot at AFDA in 2006. Life is truly just a cycle of reaching a comfortable place then falling all the way down to the bottom again. And starting over. I quickly saw that I wasn't as talented in acting as my privately schooled counterparts, and lost my love for the arts very fast. But telling my Coloured father that he had wasted R60 000 for my first year (and it was only April) didn't seem like the best idea. So, I stuck it out for 120 000 rand more.

But even though I was physically there, mentally, my mind was at parties. Actually, I wasn't even physically at college most days. I would write my name on the register and sneak out before the lecturer arrived. My friends and I would pub hop in the Lower Main Road. Student beer was 50% off – the fucking high-life for a 17-year-old. Actors and artists were genderfluid by nature and I could kiss girls and smoke weed with reckless abandon. Clubbing, drinking, letting everyone touch my private parts – the free-spirited hippie college life was very obviously meant for me.

Until it wasn't.

My Catholic guilt visited me in my sober moments and I felt ashamed of my lack of direction and my debaucherous palate. I didn't necessarily lose any of my untoward desires, but I knew it was time to go back into my closet.

I met my college boyfriend in my second year.

The house opposite my childhood home had been vacant for some time and when the new people moved in, it was glaringly obvious that they didn't fit into our predominantly Islamic, gham community.

The family, a single-child couple from Rondebosch East, spoke in a twangy, abrasive, New Apostolic accent that was condescending, even if they didn't intend it to be. Their daughter was my age and my mother said to make her feel welcome, because she had made friends with the child's mother – they jogged together, apparently. This girl was obviously still mourning her richer past life and made little effort to get close with us riff-raff. Regardless, on her birthday, she begrudgingly invited me and the rest of the Heights crew to her party. We didn't like her very much, but went anyway, because we loved parties.

And there, amidst the other normal-looking partygoers, was Jobe. He wasn't very attractive, so I ignored him and kissed his friend all night. I had no idea at the time, but his friend was a friend of my future husband. There was no chemistry between me and him and we left that night just friends. Jobe, however, took my number from him and added me on Mxit.

We chatted for a few weeks and I sort of remembered him. I think I was flattered that someone found me hot enough to go to that much effort. He was only in matric, but 17, so I wasn't weird about it. I myself was also 17.

He visited me and professed his love. We dated. I fell in love. I introduced him to my college friends and family. I spent each weekend with him for the next six months. We kissed, we made plans to get married when he graduated.

One day at college he messaged me.

'Shana, I need to tell you something. But you're going to be angry.'

I remember getting a knot in my stomach. He was going to break up with me. He had cheated. I was willing to accept any-thing besides that.

'I told you a small lie.'

'Okay.'

'Promise you won't get upset, please?'

'I promise. Just tell me.'

'I'm not 17. I'm 16.'

'What?'

'Okay, I'm not actually 16 yet.'

I was livid. I had mentally prepared myself to spend my life with this almost 18-year-old who was now telling me that I would have to wait two extra years to go clubbing with him.

Of course, I forgave him. My college friends thought that the development was both hilarious and a red flag. But red has always been my favourite colour.

We dated for the rest of the year and the December holidays. And then he started university.

Jobe stopped calling.

Now that he was in the big league, my college ass wasn't as exciting. He didn't have time to chat in the morning before class anymore. He went silent.

I had been Shannoned.

And it really messed me up.

My days felt longer than they ever had. My chest would burn with anticipation that he was going to call me and change his mind. I needed the boy I had been dating for the last year to come to his senses, but I didn't have the self-control to wait.

So I phoned him. Every morning. It was like a compulsion. I couldn't move past the morning or get out of bed without calling him. I called under the guise of just being concerned that he might oversleep for class. I would tell him I was just calling because he was still my best friend and I wouldn't call again for the day. Every day, the very thin guise was different.

But the calls weren't relieving me, because there was no enthusiasm in his voice. That special inflection that had been mine, that I had heard on every phone call, was gone. I had to hear it just one more time. I was addicted to the times when he would call me between classes.

'Shana, please don't phone me in the mornings,' he asked me one day.

I was caught off guard.

'Can I phone you this afternoon rather?'

I needed him to love me again, like he used to. He said he would love me. Did he just forget our promises? What the fuck was wrong with him. The fucking liar.

'No, Shana, yoh!' He let out a frustrated cry that I felt in my heart.

That was the first time I realised the magnitude of his repulsion. The knowledge seeped through the brick wall around my head. But I was still convinced I could change his mind.

I thought about him night and day. I stopped eating. I never slept. I hacked off my hair with a knife. I straightened it with Mediscalp and then peroxided it until it withered like ash.

I must have been a sight the next time he saw me, when he came with his mother to collect some things.

'Do you still think about me?' I asked.

He waited for his mom to get out of the car.

I asked him to stay just a bit longer and hold me, but he chose to leave. I was sad at how selfish he was being. He knew me. He knew I loved his hugs. He could have healed me.

By the second term, I had deteriorated so much that my family sent me back to a psychologist I had seen as a child. My father had found me, crying, dialling Jobe's number on the house phone. He took the phone away and scolded me for being weak and pathetic. I don't blame him, though being punished for being sad was a lesson that certainly didn't help me to seek help as an adult.

When I told the doctor about the thoughts that were plaguing me so much that I couldn't sleep at night, she suggested a two-week break at the clinic she worked at.

I agreed to go only because I realised the opportunity for pity it presented. Jobe loved me. I just knew it. If he saw me in a real hospital he would see the cruelty of his actions. There was no way a man who loved me and promised me all those things could live with himself after breaking up with me.

On my first night at the clinic, all I could think about was switching on my phone to bathe in all the messages of concern from Jobe. Now, I could tell him stories about my day, stories to make him laugh, like about the man in the common room who wanted to be near me the whole time and wouldn't let me leave. I prolonged the wait even more. I was so proud of my willpower. I undressed and got ready for bed. The nurse knocked on the door and gave me my evening meds. I showed her that I had swallowed and she left.

I climbed under the sparse covers and switched on my phone.

Nothing. No SMSes. No missed calls. No voicemails.

Okay. My stomach knotted, my breathing quickened. I opened Mxit as a last resort.

No offline messages. He was online though. On 'hot' and 'busy'.

The choice: say nothing and 'win', but risk him never speaking to me again. Or, say hello and give the power away, but lead the conversation onto just how he destroyed you. Guilt him into loving you again and trap him with it – at least he won't be with anyone else.

I said, 'Hello. You're online late, hahahaha.' It was 9pm.

Almost 15 years later, my stomach is in a knot about it as I recall my desperation to seem casual.

He didn't respond.

The medication was making me drowsy, but the calm of sleep seemed merciful. I usually couldn't fall asleep when he didn't reply, I stayed up wondering what he was doing and who he was chatting to. I did relationship math in my head, to the point where I could feel my mind physically straining as it just-just got to the precipice of the proper conclusion. I recalled every conversation we had ever had, scanning for clues about his schedule and what the most likely excuse was for his preoccupation. Hours and hours of calculations. My mind had gotten so full of webs that I had to write my thoughts down in a book. A book that filled up very quickly.

I typed, 'How are you?' I couldn't resist. The pain of being ignored was nothing compared to the compulsion to act.

His contact went grey. He had logged off. But it was late, he must have fallen asleep. He would never purposefully log off without saying goodnight to me. I was his ritual in the evenings. My sleeping tablet caressed me and my mind stilled as I drifted.

Waking up the next morning was less easy. My heart was physically hurting, no longer covered by the protective film of the narcotics. I frantically called his number to get my morning dose of him. Just a small dose, to take the edge off. His phone was off, so I just left a voicemail to remind him that I would always be there for him. It made me feel better.

I stood up and headed to the common room unshowered. Showering would force me to think about my life, it was too therapeutic. I sat down and lit a cigarette. The whole room was thick with smoke. My smoke, other people's smoke. It was like a thick blanket and I enjoyed the way it covered us all. The other people looked so crazy. I was happy that my mental state wasn't as poor as theirs. I merely loved someone, I wasn't insane like the fuckers around me.

I made a pact with myself again that I wouldn't log on, or message him again until the evening. I would stretch the hiatus from contact for as long as I could bear. I would train myself to prolong the silences between contact. Besides, it made the eventual contact sweeter, like an orgasm.

I spent the day looking for distractions.

Hours later, one missed call.

My dad. I logged onto Mxit.

No offline messages.

The tears streamed down. I lay on the bed, contorting my body in an attempt to outmove the pain that was coursing through it. I didn't scream, but I groaned loudly. I was so frustrated. I was so sore. The truth was trying to seep through the cracks of the delusion I was building and it fucking hurt.

I phoned him.

'Shana, please stop calling me.'

'Why are you being like this?' I sobbed.

'Doing what? I broke up with you.'

'But why?' I screamed into the phone. 'Why?'

'Because I don't love you anymore.'

'No. You do. You don't just stop loving people?'

Silence.

'I love you,' I said in a calm voice. The switch was sudden. I felt calm.

Silence.

'Please say something. Are you still there?'

'I dunno what to say.'

'Just say you love me.'

'I dunno what to say.' He sounded defeated.

'I'm in hospital,' I had completely forgotten to mention this. I waited to hear shock and concern in his voice.

'What happened?' It wasn't a distressed question, but he asked, so it was progress.

I made a meal of speaking to him. I explained every detail of the last two days to a quiet phone.

'Can I come see you?' he asked when I eventually stopped talking.

I gave him the details. He said he would be there the next night.

When he arrived at the clinic the next evening, I was already sitting outside on the stone bench by the fountain. He parked his red scooter. I had told my new-found asylum friends that my

86

boyfriend was coming. I planned on taking him inside to the common room, which doubled as the visiting area.

He sat down and handed me a stuffed animal he had bought me on our first Valentine's Day.

He was looking around us. 'I thought you could use her. Especially in this place.'

I didn't feel happy while he was there. I had expected to fall in love when I saw him. But again, the uncanny valley sense that something wasn't quite like I had imagined it would be stopped me from enjoying the moment.

'Shana, I came to see you to say goodbye.'

'What do you mean?'

'I can't do this anymore. You phone me every day. I'm scared to get near my phone.'

'What do you mean?' I knew what he meant. Hearing it out loud from him showed me the truth about my behaviour. My compulsion. But I didn't want to heal, because that would mean forgetting our love.

'Shana, I broke up with you almost six months ago. You haven't stopped calling me. I stopped my mom from going to the police. Please, leave me alone.'

'Why are you doing this? You didn't need to end our relationship.' I was crying loudly.

'This! This is why! This is embarrassing. Look where you are! How can I tell people my girlfriend is here?'

My brain was in a zombie state for the rest of the conversation. My mental illness descended with its full weight, uncomfortable and heavy and dark. Depression is a tangible outside force, it has a personality and a goal. I could feel the attack. It was both gradual and immediate. He left and I didn't call him again.

But a new journey had started. A journey of self. And I really wasn't fucking there for it. I spent the next day in bed. I played the conversation over and over in my head. I was too weighed down to move. It felt as if the depression was making its way through my body, via my bloodstream. When I got used to a position, it wouldn't feel as heavy. I was scared that if I moved, it would flow through me. I was scared of feeling new degrees of sadness. So I lay still. I only got up to smoke.

I don't have any memories of how I felt for the rest of that week. I did what I was supposed to. I didn't put my phone back on and I waited eagerly each day for the tranquiliser that afforded me sleep. It was the best part of each day, sleeping. Every morning the bad feelings would flood my chest and then the mountain of progress I was yet to make would flood my mind. I decided that when I got home, I would kill myself. Convinced that I was a bad seed. An unchaste, too loud, too big, too outspoken, troublesome, broken girl who couldn't be loved by anyone: not family or boys, or girls.

The day before I was meant to leave, I joined an art class and couldn't manage to match any colours. The task was to make a card for someone on the outside and I just couldn't find any patterns or colours that matched. My brain couldn't create. I sat at the table, perplexed. Just staring at the papers and sparkles and glitter in front of me. In my peripheral vision, I saw a blonde girl sit down next to me.

'Are you okay?'

'No,' it was the first time I had said it out loud. I looked up at her. In front of me, a child who could have been no older than 12 sat smiling. She was beautiful. Her eyes were blue. I forced myself to smile back and averted my eyes. I didn't want her to think I was staring at the hundreds of cuts all over her body.

'I cut myself, no one did it to me.' She must have been used to people asking. 'The girls at school are so mean.' She didn't look at me anymore. She kept crafting.

I stood up and left the room. I left everything in a mess on the table and ran up to my room. My heart was pounding. The tears were running, mixing with my sweat and mucous. I got up the stairs to my room, stumbling.

I phoned Jobe. I wasn't giving up so easily. He never answered.

When I left the clinic, my OCD and bipolar disorder stayed with me, damaging me. I spiralled into a devastating pattern of finding people who were as broken as me, who didn't know love, and I showered them with it.

Every single person left and I would have to pick up the pieces of my mind afterwards, every time.

I only slept with people I felt nothing for. Because if you don't care, it doesn't hurt.

# Chapter 7

# The end of my lyf

My head hung heavy in October 2010. I was three months shy of my 21st birthday and I had committed the one unforgivable act for a Coloured girl from the Cape Flats.

I sat on the toilet, staring at the pregnancy test, mostly confused by how I had fallen so far down the social ladder so quickly. The sex I had been having wasn't even worth the trouble I was in. But the two lines that were almost glowing in one of the darkest moments of my life were there and they weren't fading. I kept staring at them, though I don't know what I was hoping would happen. I was just too scared to look away. I do remember that it was a Sunday and that I was getting ready to go to church. If this were a text I would type LOL. My entire life could be summed up by just fucking typing LOL. At this point I had graduated college with poor results. I started working at a call centre instead of pursuing any of my actual life goals and I was dating a boy I didn't even like, because his bossy, obnoxious sister was my only work friend. And for good measure, to really give my mother that heart attack, he was Muslim. I was a Catholic, Coloured 20-year-old, who was pregnant by a 19-year-old, Muslim call centre worker I didn't like. I was for all intents and purposes, binne in my poes[1].

I had sat there for so long that I didn't need to wipe my vagina. I had drip-dried and the air had taken care of the residue. I undressed, folding the test into my dirty clothes.

---

1  This is difficult to translate directly, but it basically means, 'I was screwed'.

I stood there in the shower stream, feeling nothing but the hot water on my face making its way through the grooves of my lips, my nose. I thought of how it hit the top of my head, then meandered around it in a circle, like a waterslide at a theme park. I remember wanting the water to wash away how dirty I felt and how at one point I stood there, completely submerged, just laughing at myself.

I showered for longer than I needed to, because I knew once I exited the shower, the rest of my life would begin.

My cellphone lay on my bed as I got dressed. I kept walking towards it to call Hashiem. Each time I got to the phone, something else needed to be done. My legs needed more lotion, or I needed to brush my teeth, or find my deodorant. When I did make the call, the conversation was underwhelming.

'Hey,' he answered. I guess I had hoped for a cheerier hello. I would have liked to think that allowing him to ejaculate inside of me entitled me to at least a two-syllable greeting. 'Hey,' I said, already defeated by the day. 'I'm pregnant.'

'Okay cool. Cool.'

'Okay, I need to go to church. I'll come around later.'

'Okay cool. Cool.'

And that was it. That would forever be the first time I told someone I was carrying their baby.

Cool.

'Suffer little children to come unto me, for . . .'

Are you fucking kidding me? The church echoed with the voices of the roughly 300 congregants who were apparently there for First Holy Communion. I hadn't known that the 10am mass would be a goddamn charade and I had really just wanted to have a normal service in which I had an hour and a half of going through the motions while thinking about something else. You

91

know, the way church is supposed to go. Alas, I stood behind the back pew and watched as 20 kids processed down the aisle, holding candles. I couldn't even leave, because the fuckers who ran things at the church had seen me come in.

'Suffer little children to come unto me, for theirs is the kingdom of the lord.'

I have very little memory of the events that followed. I know that I called my cousin, who called my sister, who told my brother-in-law. From there, none of it was in my control anymore. That night I did go and see Hashiem, but it was just a brief meeting and we didn't even discuss the pregnancy. By the time a week was over, my entire family knew that I was pregnant. By six weeks I had been outed to everyone and before I could even come to terms with it, my dad put me on medical aid, my sister started gathering all of her old baby stuff from her sons and my mother hadn't spoken to me in a week. I didn't know what the fuck was happening. My sister took me to her doctor a few days later, to confirm that I was, in fact, pregnant.

'Are you keeping the baby?' I was caught off guard by this question. I hadn't even considered that there was an option. 'If not, we can deal with it here in the office,' the doctor continued. I felt their eyes on me, waiting for my decision. It actually felt strange that she was asking me and not addressing the question to my sister.

'Yes,' the Catholic inside of me answered. I was a little embarrassed to say that I would have liked to not keep the baby, but I didn't want to be forever associated with killing it. I think back to that moment quite a bit. I answered yes mostly because my sister was in the room. Had I been alone in the room with the doctor, I would have probably explored my other options. But I cared about whether or not my sister thought I was responsible, or good.

'The sac is empty,' the doctor said at my first visit to the OBGYN department at around eight weeks. This time, my mom stood next to the bed, looking on the screen. It was a bittersweet moment, which I feel guilty about now. I lay there, hoping that there would be nothing to see and that the entire pregnancy nonsense had been a scare. Everyone now knew that I wasn't a virgin, but at least without a baby, I wouldn't have to keep paying for it.

'Oh, wait ... I see it. It's just early days.'

Fuck. The nightmare was really happening.

'Congratulations, Mommy.'

I didn't realise the doctor was speaking to me. The word didn't resonate with me and I didn't know it then but it wouldn't resonate for the next few years. It seemed almost like a taunt. The doctor was so kind to me. I remember this gentle white woman touching my hand, smiling at me as we located Sidney-Jonah in my belly. My mother sat stoic in the corner. The idea that this doctor thought I was capable of taking care of another human being was incomprehensible, but she made me feel a sort of comfort. It was fleeting, but ten years later I can call that feeling up and feel it again when I need to be comforted. To be fair, I had never been told that I was capable of anything extraordinary. That sounds sadder than it is. It didn't hurt. It just was.

'I just want to fetch your printout, I'll be back shortly.' The lady left the room and the tears ran down into my ears.

I lay there in my mother's silence.

'The sac is empty,' I tried to break the silence with something, anything. That seemed like the most positive thing to say at that moment.

'Jy's pregnant, Shana,' she cut me off. Her anger was so tangible, so thick.

93

I tried to think about other things while we waited for the doctor to come back, but my mind kept throwing embarrassing memories to the forefront. 'I should have been a doctor' was one of them. When I was a child, my daddy always said I was smart enough to be a doctor. In his mind, this was the highest honour. A doctor was the peak of learned. Not a doctor of anything, though. In those days, Coloured people didn't really understand that a doctorate could be in any field until there was a sort of local awakening in the 2010s. To my dad, a doctor helped sick people feel better and he was going to father one. He was very vocal about how proud of me he would be if I studied medicine. Lying there, it dawned on me that now, that wasn't a possibility anymore. I was going to be a mother. Single mothers can't have good-girl careers. We fornicated our chances away. Bear in mind, I wasn't even studying medicine, or planning to; but now that I was pregnant, there wasn't even an option. Any prospect of having anything other than the life I knew was gone.

On my 21st birthday, I was three months pregnant. I didn't expect any sort of celebration. In the week leading up to the day, I could feel a fear-induced nausea making its home in my stomach. I was nauseous most of the time because of hyperemesis, but this nausea felt different. I dreaded the idea of seeing anyone on or around my birthday and having them either ask me what I did to celebrate or avoid the subject as it hung in the air. When the day finally arrived, I spent most of the morning hiding in my room. Leaving my room meant that my family would know I was awake and would wish me happy birthday. Except, they wouldn't mean it.

Around 10am, the electric garage door below my bedroom opened. When it didn't close again, I peered out the window.

'Something's Tables and Chairs Hire', I could have projectile

94

vomited against the glass. A group of young Muslim men carried white plastic chairs and disassembled trestle tables from the branded truck into our garage. Oh no.

'Shana, wil jy nou slaap tot die son in jou gat in skyn?'[2] My mother could have her own fucking merch with that line printed across every item. I didn't answer. I stayed in my room some more. But my family had now stopped operating in hushed tones and the commotion outside my room almost guaranteed that they knew I was awake and avoiding them. My mom came up my stairs.

'Gat was vir jou. Die mense gat 2 o' clock hier wies'. That was it: get up and wash, people are coming. That was the equivalent of her wishing me 'Happy Birthday'. I accepted it, graciously.

Outside, I watched as the people set up the birthday party I didn't want. My sister and her husband were there. My older cousins, who I didn't really care for, were there too. I felt that everyone was expectant of my gratitude as they set up chairs and laid out the chicken platters. I stood in the centre of it all, watching my family use my birthday as a way to save face with our relatives.

By the evening, everyone I knew had arrived, even my baby daddy. I was so angry that he was there. At this point in my pregnancy, everything he did was fucking stupid. I hated the smell of miang stokkies and Maca oil that seemed to seep out from every pore of his body. It made me so sick and angry that I couldn't stand being around him. He looked nothing and was nothing like the man I had believed I would marry. He couldn't even drive.

---

2    This is another one of those phrases that are difficult to translate directly. It literally means, 'Are you gonna lie there sleeping till the sun shines out your hole?', which is to say, basically, 'Are you going to lie there sleeping all day?'

We had met in a call centre. A job I had only been meant to occupy until my acting career took off. He was a reminder of how I had mixed with the lower classes and he was a symbol of my horniness. Also, my hormones were volatile. (Yes, I am aware that I was an absolute classist tool).

The evening was tense but not unbearable. Everyone ate finger foods and drank alcohol. Besides me. I couldn't even have any champagne during my own toast. But I wasn't as sad as I had been when I woke up, until the speeches. My dad chose not to say anything. My mother took the floor, though, and thanked everyone for coming, 'even under the circumstances'.

'Dankie dat julle almal gekom het. Is nou nie die beste occasion nie, but os sal ma die beste daarvan maak. Die lewe is mos maar soe.'

It wasn't the best occasion but we'll make the most of it. Life is just like that.

I wanted the earth to swallow me into its core and never again reopen.

But this wasn't the worst of it. As the next few weeks passed, my hyperemesis peaked. I can still clearly remember the first time I vomited. I was in my room watching TV. The room started spinning, but not in circles. I guess it was more like a rocking back and forth, as if I was on a boat. My mouth started to water. I made it to the toilet just in time to slam dunk my breakfast straight into the water. But what I hadn't anticipated was that my bladder would release simultaneously. I vomited until my stomach cramped from contracting. The bathroom floor was colder than it had ever been. I had spent some time on it after nights of heavy partying and drinking; but this was the loneliest it had ever felt.

**hyperemesis**

/hʌɪpəˈrɛməsɪs/

noun

MEDICINE

  1. *severe or prolonged vomiting.*
  'the clinical practicability is limited by a higher degree of side effects, especially hyperemesis'

  ○ persistent severe vomiting leading to weight loss and dehydration, as a condition occurring during pregnancy.

noun: **hyperemesis gravidarum**

  'hyperemesis gravidarum occurs in approximately 0.5 to 2 per cent of pregnancies'

Ain't that some shit. When it rains, it rains vomit.

When I was four months pregnant, I broke up with Hashiem. It was my decision. In the four months prior, there had been certain developments that depressed me, or at least added to my depression. His parents asked me to no longer come to their home until I agreed to either turn Muslim, or have a paternity test. His mother had cornered me one afternoon when I went to pick him up to go shopping for the baby.

'A man phoned here yesterday, did Hashiem tell you?' The smugness in her voice made me want to punch her, more than I usually wanted to punch the bitch.

'No, Mrs Laattoe, he didn't say anything to me. Phoned about what?'

'He says the baby might be his. His name starts with a J, can't remember now.'

One would think to jot down something that important. We stood in silence. She stared me down, wide eyed. I was at a loss for words. I was back in that counsellor's room at high school.

'I, um. I don't know who that could be.'

'Well, that's what he said.'

I didn't enter his house again until I messaged him saying that I felt indifferent about our relationship.

I went through the rest of my pregnancy alone. I had two friends who were pregnant at the same time as me. One was married and the other lived with her boyfriend. I amplified these facts in my loneliness. I still think pregnancy is a team activity, or at least it should be. The world has this romantic idea of the creation of life in the womb. Yes, women are magical creatures who can endure immense pain and bounce back from labour almost instantly, ready to bear the brunt of inadequate men and intolerable children, but I honestly believe that gestation is romanticised in order to make it easier to ignore the true suffering pregnant women endure. By now I have had both single pregnancies and a pregnancy with a dedicated partner by my side. Physically all were equally excruciating; but I can say with absolute conviction that there is nothing positive to be said about being pregnant without someone at your side for support. And yes, the person by your side needs to be the other, equally responsible party who is biologically and emotionally invested in the foetus, or it just doesn't fucking mean as much.

With my first pregnancy, my mother accompanied me to most of my prenatal visits. She meant well; I see that now as I grab these memories from a very deep, sore place buried in my psyche. But I can see vividly in my mind's eye the older, better women lined up along the pastel blue and yellow walls, sitting next to their husbands and boyfriends. Each one of them was a contrast to me. They seemed better in the way they moved, the way they existed. More sophisticated. More validated. They read the courtesy magazines more gracefully. They leaned back in their chairs, unbothered. Grown. I was aware of how they looked at me with side glances. I was young. My mother shouldn't have had to be dragged along to fill the void of a baby daddy. How dare I tarnish her golden years with such nonsense? I felt like a pariah. Rightfully so.

In essence, I vomited alone and pulled back my own hair as I wiped my mouth. I endured my cravings alone; no one was responsible for my whims. My 1am craving for Zinger wings wasn't a cute anecdote that I could laugh about with my significant other. It was now a dreaded occurrence that I had to endure, instead of experience.

I woke up one morning, absolutely lussing for chocolate.

I mentioned it casually to my mom, who answered with a scathing 'Jy moet nou 'n man gehad het wat vir jou kan chocolate koep. Maar jy hettie eers dit nie.'

I smiled, although I would have collapsed if I had given in to the pain that spread through my chest as the words exited her mouth. I was well aware that I was single.

Most people said whatever they wanted to about my 'situation'. My actions were akin to those of a scoundrel in court, or a criminal in the newspaper. They spoke at me, not to me. And they said shit they thought I didn't already know. I really didn't need anyone to tell me that my situation sucked; I was right there, in the vacuum.

On Father's Day 2010, I was 37 weeks along. Although my gynae had convinced me to undergo a caesarean at 40 weeks, I was nervous as the prospect of going into labour approached. My mother had been responsible for my pregnancy plan up until this point. I felt more like a child going through with my parents' wishes for their grandchild than a woman who was about to give birth to her own baby.

By this time, my mom had prepared my room, thrown a baby

99

shower without inviting any of my friends, bought the baby's clothes and toiletries and set up all of the swings, bouncy chairs and camper cots I had received from my sister. She had even packed my hospital bag. But we were three weeks away, so it was all just on pre-standby.

My family sat around the table, enjoying the rare winter afternoon sun that was beaming, almost blindingly, through the glass double doors between our porch and living room. It was hotter than it had been for a while and our home was the venue for the occasion, chosen so we could all enjoy the pool in our sleepwear (like the trashy, new-money Coloured folk we are) just one more time before winter started. My sister and her family were there, her two babies pulled close to the table in their highchairs. My aunty, cousins and my mom and dad were on the other side. I was in the centre by the roasted potatoes. I had chosen that chair specifically because it was easy to manoeuvre in and out to run to the toilet. My bladder was basically a water balloon with a hole in it. But this day was particularly bad. It could feel the urine dripping through my clenched muscles. I couldn't really enjoy my food.

'Jy pee darem baie,' my mom said over the chicken. Inappropriate as it was to make a public observation about peeing, in my family it was okay, because it was about me.

'I can't stop, my pad is wet,' I replied, fully aware that I was oversharing. At nine months pregnant I had to wear a pad every day or the discharge would swirl down my mutton-like thighs.

I hadn't had many lessons on the anatomy, failing Bio and all in Grade 10 so badly that I had to swap it out for Art, Standard Grade. I was expecting a gush of water to fire-hose out of my vagina when my water broke, so I ignored the trickle until it got wider and more forceful.

Our guests went home at around 8pm, when I finally told my mom that I thought I needed the hospital. The water had soaked through the pad and wet my pants on the outside. We drove there fairly slowly. My mother didn't seem to have the same sense of urgency as I. It reminded me of the time my dad had a stroke and she got dressed and tidied the kitchen before we rushed him to the ICU.

Private hospital was a walk in the park. I was admitted as soon as I explained what had been happening for the last 24 hours. In ten minutes I was hooked up to the machines, beeping. My mom was on the chair in the corner of the triage room. The round white analogue clock hung above the bed: 9pm. I couldn't stop checking the time. It was actually quite insignificant. But that is my clearest memory of that night. The gynaecologist walked in a few minutes later and checked the notes. He felt my stomach and smiled at me.

'Who is more impatient, you or the baby?' he said jokingly. I didn't really like him. He was an old, white man with a weird, powdery smell. He had the same calm, pompous sureness that most white people had. He hadn't made it a secret that he was surprised by my age and that I had no business being pregnant. He also kept saying he knew my sister. I guess that information kept me in line. Because I was young. Apart from that very first female doctor, the physicians I encountered in my pregnancy didn't speak of my baby with enthusiasm. I accepted that, but it didn't make the pregnancy easier. For some reason people thought they needed to inform me that I was fucked. He wasn't outright rude, but he wasn't outright kind.

It annoyed me, but he was a doctor. My sister had suggested him, because she had given birth with his partner physician.

I smiled in response to his question. I always felt the need to

101

be coy when speaking to a doctor. My parents always addressed them with reverence and shyness. It must have rubbed off.

'Okay. You're definitely at the start of labour.' He made a note. 'We can take him out in the morning.'

He smiled. I smiled. We all smiled. He left.

My mom said goodbye and that she would be there in the morning, first thing. For the rest of the night I lay there awake, drifting in and out of fear. I had been stressed about being pregnant for so long that I didn't really consider that it wasn't forever; or that there would actually be a baby. I mean, I knew. But I didn't really know.

At 7:30am, my mother came into the ward followed by the nurse. I had never been as happy to see my mother's face. The last ten hours had been the loneliest of my life. My phone was a small distraction from the constant anxious knowledge that this was the last time in my whole life that I would be a young girl. Tomorrow I would be a mother. No one was chatting to me in any case. All my friends and cousins were at the World Cup celebrations in the CBD, or singing 'Waka Waka' at their own private parties. And I was lying alone, waiting for my son to arrive.

At 8am, they wheeled me into the theatre.

I hadn't expected so many people to be in the room. My mom was being prepped outside. She was going to 'catch the baby', a role usually reserved for the father. I hadn't even considered calling Hashiem. My mother would have been angry if I took the moment away from her. I lay there, waiting for the dreaded lower body paralysis the doctor explained would happen after the injections in my spine.

The team of doctors sat around me as I lay on the operating table. My mom walked in and rested her hand on my shoulder. It felt good.

'Okay, we are making the first incision,' the doctors spoke to each other at the end of the table. I felt so small, looking into the light above my head. They hadn't really addressed me and it felt as if everything was happening around me without me. They discussed procedure and other personal things around me as they worked.

'Okay, last push,' my gynae joked.

Just, at the time I wasn't sure if he was kidding. I wasn't a doctor, I hadn't had a baby before. For all I knew they needed me to push. So I obliged as best I could.

'Push, push,' they all chanted, mockingly.

I know now they were making fun, but I tried to clinch and push, just in case they were serious.

My face contorted and they giggled, but kept it up. My baby emerged as they were making fun of me. They handed him straight to my mother.

'Hello Sidney,' she said to him.

The first voice he heard wasn't mine. And then, there it was. I was a mother. Sort of.

I had made the overnight transition from child to parent, with nothing in between. But because I was unwed and lived at home, it wasn't really my baby and I still wasn't a grown-up. I wasn't the authority and so my child was not to answer to me, but to them (and I was to listen to any older family member or family friend who had unsolicited advice and unwarranted expertise in what was best for my child). My parents bought me a car, only to be used for the baby's needs: clinic visits, crèche drop-offs.

I couldn't even go out with Sidney if my parents didn't agree. He was another chain to keep me in my parents' house. I had dreamed for so long of the day I would turn 21 and my mom could no longer dictate my comings and goings, only to have a baby mere months before my goal.

I couldn't go for job interviews. I couldn't go to auditions.

'Toe jy moet audition toe loep haal jy 'n baby,' my dad would say whenever I even broached the idea.

I started to believe that my whole purpose was to sit in my room with my child. The idea seemed to stretch for an eternity. Day in and day out I sat with, nursed, stared at this child, without feeling anything. At least, I didn't feel anything positive. The days and weeks blurred. The expression is a cliché, but I remember those days all merged into a silent, painful montage. There was a lot of quiet crying and staring at him. I wanted him to die in his cot so badly. One morning, the anxiety and sadness was so overwhelming that I chose to stay in bed longer than usual. I felt the pain in my throat just sit there. That cramping feeling that happens when you try to swallow emotion. It wouldn't go back down and just made home in my lymph nodes as I physically tried to gulp them down. Sidney was sleeping next to me on the bed. He was so tiny. I looked at him, but instead of anger, that morning I felt sorry for him. God had given him me as a mother. I had nothing. I was nothing. He was a bastard child to an unwed, unemployed laaitie. What a shitty hand the world had played him. I turned on my back and stared at the ceiling, relieved that he hadn't woken up yet. My mother walked in and peered in through the chink in the curtain that hung next to my bed.

'Kom, staan op en maak skoon. You need to get this place cleaned up.'

'He's still sleeping, Mommy. We were up last night late.'

'So?' she had a smirk on her lips. She was enjoying this.

'I am very tired,' I responded.

'Of course, is jy tired, Shana. But iemand van jou stature kannie net lê nie.'

The sniffle that accompanied her giggle pushed me over the edge. It ignited something inside of me though. I wanted to be better. It chipped away at a layer of something which at the time I couldn't pinpoint.

Eventually, I started to feel Hashiem's absence. By now he hadn't come forward or tried to make contact with his child as I had assumed he would. I knew he hated me, but I had this fantastic notion that men were proud of their offspring. In his absence, I had started to grow fonder of him. Or perhaps the thought of being with someone who couldn't discriminate against me for conceiving Sidney seemed more appealing than it had when I was pregnant and angry. My indignation at his radio silence turned into desperation. I kept checking my Blackberry for a message or missed call. A voicemail would have been exactly the romantic gesture it took for me to fall back into his arms and no longer be a single mom. But nothing happened. So I made the first move.

'Hey.'

He didn't recognise the number, I just knew it.

'It's Shana. The baby is born.'

'I know ja. Iptishaam saw it on Facebook.'

It.

'Oh. So why didn't you visit?'

'You said you didn't wanna be with me, so I left you alone, Shana.'

'I didn't say you can't see the baby.'

'What's his name?'

He didn't even know our child's name.

'Sidney.'

'Oh. He's not Muslim.'

Why would he be?

'No, not yet.' I don't know why I said that. I do know why I said that; but I didn't mean it. 'Can we set up a meeting or something?'

'I have a girlfriend.' I was not expecting that. Even though I never loved him, I immediately felt threatened by the idea of this woman who was now higher on his list of priorities than me and his child. What an absolute bitch.

'That doesn't matter. This is about Sidney.' That was my 'in'.

'Yeah okay, sure.'

'What time should I come around?'

'Not today, I have plans today.'

'Tomorrow?' even I could hear my desperation.

'Sure.'

'Okay cool.'

'Cool.' He ended the call.

The next morning Sidney and I made our way to Ottery to meet his daddy. We were dressed up for our first real outing. This was a meaningful occasion, albeit a trek through Cape Town in the heart of winter. Sidney was born on 21 June and six weeks later, the rain was pouring down. I vaguely remember that there were hailstorms that year. It was icy, but Sid and I were on a mission. When I pulled up to the house, the rain had subsided. When we were dating, Hashiem would open the front door as soon as I was in the driveway, so I knew he could see me through the massive lounge window. I assumed he would be waiting, ready to open the door quickly so that I could get Sidney inside, out of the rain. So I waited in the car for a few minutes. Eventually, I left Sid and went to knock on the door. An uninspired 'coming' penetrated the wood. When he opened the door, he didn't even look up at me. It was a 'by-the-way' action performed as he chatted on his phone.

Once Sidney and I were inside, I felt slightly more hopeful. We didn't venture into his room but sat down on the couches in the front room reserved for guests. I understood that. I declined coffee.

'So, this is him, wow,' he smiled.

I handed Sidney over.

For once, I didn't have that nagging feeling that I would need to take him back again when the person who was holding him grew tired. It was permitted for me to be sitting down and resting now, his father was holding him. I now had a taste of the smugness the other women experienced when their babies were 'with dad'. I hadn't experienced that in six weeks, in fact not ever.

'I can't sit long. My girlfriend is coming after work,' he said mid casual conversation. I tried my best to keep my expression stoic and unperturbed.

'Cool.'

He sat staring at Sidney.

'So, what is going to happen now?' I asked.

'Well, I have a new job. So I can help with nappies and things.'

'Thank you. I haven't started looking for work yet. I'm still healing.'

'Natural birth?'

'No.'

'Okay.'

'Yeah.'

'Uhm, when do you want to see him again? I can bring him to see your mom them when they here?'

He looked at me and smiled, politely.

'I'll ask them.' That didn't feel very sincere.

'Okay.'

'Okay.'

The social cue was clear. I packed Sidney's things into his baby bag and took him back into my arms. At that moment, the rain started falling again, crashing loudly onto the rooftop. I was already standing. I didn't see him motion for me to sit back down, because he didn't do that. 'It's raining. I don't want him to get wet on the way to the car.' I turned back to the settee.

He put his hand on my side to steer me. At first, the gesture seemed caring. He hadn't touched me in so long. No one had. All the months of my pregnancy I had been completely without physical affection. I leaned into his hand with my hip, but that only made it more obvious that I was being pushed, handled.

'My girlfriend is really on her way,' He was still trying to be polite.

Only this time, I understood exactly what that meant.

I walked slowly towards the door. He kept his hand on me just in case, I guess. He opened the door and his steering became a little firmer. The rain was still plummeting down when my foot crossed the threshold. I walked forward, still under the afdak. I turned around to ask if he wanted to kiss Sidney goodbye. He had already closed the door behind me.

My tears fell as I drove home. Sidney was asleep, oblivious to what had happened. My heart was literally, physically large and heavy, the weight in my chest straining against whatever was holding my body together.

But besides the rejection that seemed to cover me like a thick blanket, I felt fired up. Motivated. I felt strong-ish. Determined.

A week later, after not hearing from him, I called. He rejected the call, but texted me his work email address. I emailed and he said that he 'couldn't handle this right now'. And so, for the last ten years I have handled it for us both.

Okay, perhaps that is a bit premature. It wasn't that cut and dried, but the purpose of this memoir is not to highlight the failures of a 21-year-old boy who wasn't ready to be a father. It is about my own journey in navigating an anti-female terrain. This part of my story in particular taught me that as a woman your timeline for deciding what you are ready to handle is less forgiving. Roles reversed, had a 21-year-old Coloured female left her baby in the hands of another person and said 'I am not ready to handle this right now,' she would have been burned at the stake. It was and is still mostly unheard of for a woman to up and leave her child, no matter the emotional, physical and mental abuse she had to endure from her community, strangers and everyone on the goddamn internet for being the one who stayed.

When I say that the rejection of having Hashiem denounce his child and having people brandish me a failure motivated me, I meant that it made me want more than I had; I wanted a job like my sister had, I wanted a man to love me and I wanted my parents to see me flourish.

I went back to college to study journalism and didn't tell anyone I had a child. I threw myself into learning how to write and becoming the best at it. I won an internship and started my first blog and set my sights on being more. But I was lonely. And as I threw myself into college, I also felt a longing for the youth I never had and now would never have. The rejection from my peer circle who were living it up, as 20-somethings should, left me depleted.

Now I was a young mother, men didn't look at me the same. Guys who had previously been interested seemed disappointed. The boys who had futures spoke to me with pity, or irritation. I was a waste of their time, instead of a prospect.

I started to spend time with people from my neighbourhood, drinking and smoking and doing whatever I wanted, while I left Sidney at home with my parents. I couldn't see him without feeling angry. I wanted to be free. I wanted to have fun. I wasn't a mommy. Sidney's love wasn't the type of love I craved. And here, in the throes of postnatal depression, I met Lyle.

# Chapter 8

# The one about Lyle

Okay. I think I have given you enough backstory to understand where exactly my head was when I met Lyle Eyden. I was a broken, confused mess with a baby and an inferiority complex. And I wanted to be loved. I really, really wanted to be loved. By anyone. Anyone besides my son.

That year, doing my studies, I got used to a kind of freedom. I was doing something 'official', so my parents put my son in crèche at their expense and my days were free. I didn't tell my classmates that I had a child. I relished in the one space I wasn't a mommy. To my peers I was just a student. I could smoke entjies on the common area steps and play pool in the cafeteria. I was free for a few hours a day. Nobody there pitied me. But in the evenings, I drove home and fetched my son at crèche and the long night would start. I'd have to juggle studying and homework and spend time with an active, relentless toddler. I dreaded going home.

One day class ended early, but I didn't feel motivated to make the trek back home just yet. I sat on the wooden benches outside and while I scrolled through Facebook on my Blackberry, I came across a picture of Lyle.

I stopped my scrolling to stare at this topless, chiselled man standing in front of a mirror. He was swollen and shiny. The caption was something about sending his pics to Markham Man for modelling. I was enamoured. I clicked his profile so I could devour any other images of him I could find. He was gorgeous. I felt butterflies just looking at him – and then I immediately felt disappointed that I would not have a chance. It made me angry, even. But with the anger, I felt an inkling of determination. I had watched enough romcoms to know that if I befriended a man and he fell for me 'organically' before meeting my kid, I might just end up a wife after all. I don't know what gave me the courage, if my courage was amped up by studying again, or if I was bored and needed a challenge . . . but I went to his inbox to shoot my shot.

I texted him first – and he never let me forget it for the rest of his life.

Pretty soon Lyle and I would chat every day. I peppered the chats with words like 'bra' and 'ou broe'. The more casual I kept it, the less invested I seemed. The less invested I seemed, the less embarrassing it would be when he didn't fall in love with me. And after a few weeks of back and forth, we became real friends. We moved our chats to BBM and that just made it seem more real, official. He was a great friend. He asked me to be his best friend fairly quickly which should have been the first red flag. But it felt like a trophy.

Lyle confided in me about deeply personal things very early on. He grew up a single child to a single mother. His father, a gangster who chose the thug life and never chose him. I learned that he was my Facebook friend because we had attended the same church and had even gone to school together at some point. He was two years younger than me. He had been expelled from Muizenberg High School and had to enroll in Strandfontein High in Grade 9. He identified this as taking a 'step down' and believed that it directly affected the course of his life.

112

He repeated the year but never fully recovered from the embarrassment. As the years went on, Lyle felt the deficit of having a single mom who worked for a mediocre salary, while his cousins and friends came from more well-off, co-parent homes (his sentiments, not mine). He couldn't go to university or afford the same clothes as the other boys. What he lacked in privilege he made up for in being the life of the party. He also very aware that his smile was kryptonite to a Coloured girl. But the boys never liked him; and the girls never wanted him for more than sex. His story made me pity him. I was privileged, regardless of my fucked-up family. A deep desire to fix him up possessed me. In the weeks that followed I was his rock and he was mine. Also, he was a Catholic. I would have hit the tollie jackpot if I landed this one.

Every morning I would change my profile picture to signal that I was awake and he would greet me. We chatted from morning till night. He told me I was beautiful and that I was a great mother – information that was both inaccurate and that he could never have known from our limited interactions. He reassured me that my parents were wrong about me and my choices and that Hashiem was crazy for leaving his child behind. We spoke about everything.

For a long time he never asked to meet in person.

And then it happened.

The evening I actually met Lyle was strange. It is somewhat supernatural and unbelievable, I suppose – but I swear it occurred as I tell it. As part of my college bravado, I had started to go out more and lie to my parents about projects and study groups. I did shit like join the church band just to have an excuse to leave the house. One evening my friends and I were at a party in Lentegeur – me, under the guise of being dedicated to the Lord. To be fair, some members of my church were in attendance, but more to fuck and party than praise and worship (it wasn't a Sunday). We braaied and drank beers and around 8pm I checked my phone.

'What you doing?' I messaged. I was tipsy.

'Aweh, Shana. Just lamming with a half bottle of whiskey, you?'

'At a party with Linda and Terry. Met a bra named "Smeerwors" earlier, that kind of vibe.'

'LOL, are the kinnes reg? Come fetch me.'

I wasn't sure if he was joking till he gave his address. Intoxicated, I climbed into the passenger seat of my car and Linda drove. Terry and three other people loaded into the back of my tiny green Chery QQ3. As we ventured up Spine Road, laughing in drunken stupor, I noticed a woman standing on the pavement opposite the road from the famous Total Garage on the corner of Spine and Weltevreden. I can still see her clearly in my mind. She wore a white gown, the same as one would wear in a hospital. She wasn't scary looking, but I knew that she was out of place in the busy street. She stood still, arms hanging at her side. When I focused on her, the sound of the party faded. I couldn't hear the traffic. The only thing that broke the trance was Linda saying 'Oh my God, did you guys see that girl?'

Everyone looked back and said 'what girl'. I looked back and the street was empty.

'I saw her,' I said, sort of laughing, sort of scared.

'What the fuck?' Linda laughed too.

'What are yous talking about?' Terry was on a high.

No one else saw her, but I realised afterwards that no one else had needed to.

'I'm outside.' He walked out before I sent the message.

'He is kak reg,' Linda whispered before he got into the car. She had just been dumped by her boyfriend for the 100th time and was on a mission to fuck out her frustration on a rebound. So that she felt she had one up on her ex before crawling back to him. Apparently, relationships worked on a point system – the more you fuck up, the more you're winning the game.

Back at the party, Lyle and Linda flirted and I pretended to encourage their fling. He didn't ignore me; he actually made an effort to spend time with his 'best friend'. I accepted it – I had a laaitie, so I was no longer a contender. We had a lekker time. We drank and laughed and around 11pm we took the party back to Terry's house because all the free alcohol was up.

Renzo, one of the guys with us, was also a cutie. We flirted with each other sometimes, but I didn't really like him as much as Lyle. Still, he was a party-fiend and smarter than most men I had met. He seemed mysteriously clued up on many things my gham friends didn't understand, so we clicked very quickly – and very well. He was a serial dater, with a contact list of women all willing to drop trou at the click of a send button. He and Lyle didn't seem to click from the get-go. We drank some more. Linda and Lyle sat in the corner in their own convo and Terry and Renzo and I sat on the mat, getting drunker and hornier. By 1am I messaged my mom a lie I can't remember and switched off my phone.

I started kissing Terry to impress the boys.

'Are we gonna have a threesome?' Terry caught me off guard, but I didn't show it. Linda wasn't impressed by the turn of events, but I acted cool as a cucumber. I wanted them all to think I was fun.

'I wanna go home soon, Shana,' she said from the other side of the room. Lyle was beside her, smiling.

'I drank too much to drive.' I did, but I wasn't feeling drunk. I didn't want the night to end. 'I will take her,' he looked at me, mischievous, trying his luck.

'Okay. Bring my car back when you are done,' I heard myself say. I don't know why I said it.

'I can fetch you in the morning?' His hubris sat uncomfortably with me. I didn't like that he was comfortable with taking someone else's car – I had banked on him declining, actually.

'I'm gonna take her, go sleep and then fetch you when you're ready,' he smiled.

I accepted.

Lyle and Linda Left. I sat on the bed and watched Renzo and Terry kiss and undress. Terry kissed me and when the lights went out, I kissed her body, fully emersed in the lesbian fantasy I had suppressed for the last decade. I enjoyed the way Renzo watched, in awe. He was obviously glad to be alive. I had only known Terry from church, so every advance I made was a risk that I had gone too far.

Renzo watched as I went down on her. When he couldn't handle being idle any longer, he grabbed me and he and I started having sex. Then, he stopped abruptly and put his face into my shoulder.

'I can't do this.' He sounded sincerely sorry.

'What's wrong?' I didn't enjoy engaging in conversation with people while they were penetrating me, but we had an audience and I wanted to be cool. My persona had moved from a mirage of chastity to pretending I was sexually liberated and cool. Everything was a go.

'I just can't. Performance anxiety.' He pulled out and sat up straight.

'Come, we smoke a entjie,' Terry lit one, like a miang stokkie to smudge out the awkwardness.

We smoked, all naked, devastatingly sober now.

'Come we try again,' she directed her intentions at Renzo. She kissed me, kissed him and they had full-blown sex on the bed as

I watched. I lit several entjies, unsure if I was supposed to get dressed or just watch, naked. They started dating after this, but that's as far as I would like to take this particular story.

Lyle returned at around 7am. I dropped him at home and we sat in the car as I freshened up a bit. He brought me some body spray, bubble gum and other things that made me even more convinced that he was a chivalrous knight and not a vuilgat who had just scored my friend and taken my car for a joyride. I learned years later that he hadn't gone home that night after dropping Linda, but went to Fusion, instead. A club in Ottery he would later assault me at. We sat in the car for an hour, chatting and laughing. I told him about what had happened with Terry and Renzo. We laughed about it. He admitted that the story made him very horny. Then, he asked me if I wanted to come into his house, but the guilt of leaving my mom all night with Sidney was sitting on my chest. I went home.

For the next few weeks I acted as his wingman, to help him get into Linda's pants. She rejected him. She told me he gave her 'vibes'. I laughed, annoyed at her pickiness.

'He's not for me, Shana,' she would say.

'He's okay for you, but not for me, you know what I mean?'

I agreed. I actually understood, but in retrospect I am kak offended. Still, she enjoyed the attention and allowed him to shower her with it. Linda was just a massive fucking ego.

The three of us would go places and hang out every day. I didn't mind their flirting and had given up on him falling for me. He showed deep interest in her and even confided in me that he was in love with her. Again, this was a little weird because they had known each other for the better part of three weeks, but I saw it as sweet, romantic that a man was so 'in touch with his feelings'.

117

Soon Linda got back together with her cheating ex and Lyle and I became a twosome again. He visited me and we chilled for hours. I followed him to his friends' places. He played with Sidney, always showing up with ice cream or something lekker. When he could get the bakkie from his work, he would pick me up after college. We got really close, even closer than before. He didn't seem to be upset about Linda and we soon forgot about their 'moment'.

Our friendship evolved fast and I loved it.

When he kissed me on New Year's Day the next year, I was back to imagining our potential future. It felt like the perfect story: Friends who became friends with benefits – then lived happily ever after.

So I seduced him.

From that night, we started sleeping together 'for fun'. Casually. I figured that the rest would just fall into place. Naturally, people who slept together start to develop feelings – I'd seen it in the many romance movies I had watched as a teen.

After my graduation, he asked me to be his girlfriend. I started working and he quit his job. He said he did it to 'find something that pays him what he deserves', but I did find it strange that he didn't tell me what he was planning. He sort of just decided that he didn't enjoy his job anymore. I guess I was fine with it at first because I convinced myself that he was going to look for something more 'high-brow' and that he wanted us to be serious.

(Why would he care what job he had, if he didn't intend to eventually work to support us?)

But now that we were dating and I had made a commitment to being his woman, for now the expenses of everything fell on me.

I noticed that he never seemed to make any real moves to find work, only promises. He seemed comfortable with me footing the bill and buying the beers – he even offered on my behalf when we were in company. I accepted it all, because we were best friends who had fallen in love.

I took it upon myself to find him a job and he was okay with that. I wrote up his CV. Made an email address for his applications (his was unfortunately SabbyKing90@gmail.com) and sent applications for him every day. He didn't seem to 'feel' any of the jobs that called him back for an interview. I wasn't gonna force him, but I was anxious every time I mentioned that he had an interview – I could feel the resentment a bit for every time he said 'Naai, that's not for me'.

But we were in love and I was going to get him straight. He had chosen me even though I had a laaitie – I owed it to him to stay when it was rough.

Also, I didn't just fall in love with him, I fell in love with his free, fun lifestyle.

He had friends in Strandfontein who would throw parties at the drop of a hat. Everyone was always drinking and vibing. He was popular for the amount he could drink. The Village, as Strandfonteiners like to call their own area, knew him as 'Sabbyking'. To 'sabby' was their rendition of the slang word 'suip'. He was a legend as far as I knew. He knew so many of the boys who were popular at my old high school. Lyle was the party ou. And I, I was Lyle's kin. But being 'the ou' meant keeping up a certain level of bravado and aggression that I was naive to assume was only pitted against other men. He started to be a bit more commanding with me, especially in front of his friends. These were the same people we would hang out with when we were just friends, so I wasn't unfamiliar with them – which made his sudden change in behaviour strange.

I asked him about why he changed his personality when he

spoke to me in front of others and he gave me a random non-response about showing the guys I am his. He said he knew what type of girl I was because the night we met, I had had a threesome and allowed him to take my car, even though I didn't really know him. He said I was reckless and he didn't want his brasse to take advantage of me. They were scared of him and if they knew I was his, they wouldn't try anything. He wasn't necessarily awful, so I didn't want to fight about it and spoil the vibe. I guessed that he was right – I didn't exactly make the best first impression. So I just agreed and let him be.

The first time I saw his true capacity for violence in our relationship was when a friend of his invited us out clubbing. We had been dating for about a month. I wore a skimpy black dress that I had borrowed from one of Lyle's friends. I wanted to look extra sexy. It was our first club date and I had lost the baby weight, so I was in a great mood, ready to have a good time. When I walked out in my heels and get-up, his friends complimented me. I felt how my cheeks glowed and I waited for Lyle to say something. He didn't even smile at me. He just said 'I'm gonna naai you tonight', out loud. He said it in front of everyone who was with us –and that was it, that was the compliment. I giggled over how sorely disappointed and embarrassed I was. But the boys laughed and the girls woo'd. I quickly adopted a 'when in Rome' attitude.

The drive was quiet. We took my car and he insisted that he would drive. He had done that a lot since we were dating; he was the guy so he did the driving. I pretended I preferred it, but I didn't like that he thought the car was ours and not mine. I didn't even have the option to drive it anymore, which felt weird.

We arrived at the club around 11ish. It was already pretty lit and all his friends were there on the balcony outside. They called to him as we walked up and he grabbed my hand. His grab was tighter than usual. Another compliment, I thought. I paid for us to enter.

As the night progressed, he ordered rounds off my account, without checking with me first. I went up to the bar to get a drink of my own a few hours in. Before ordering, I saw an old friend, Chris, standing a few people to my left. He waved and we exchanged a quick hello. Chris and I had previously worked together at the call centre where I had met Sidney's biological father. It was nice to bump into someone familiar, especially now that I was doing better. I ordered my drink and got one for Lyle too.

'Your drinks are already paid for,' the bartender smiled at me.

'By who?' It was Chris.

I walked back to the couches where Lyle and a few of our friends sat. Of course, I proudly shared with him that my drinks were comped by Chris. I thought he'd find endless joy in it. He smiled at me, but the way he shifted quickly back to the other conversation, averting his eyes from me, was strange. I stayed on the couch all night. Lyle didn't ask me to, but his annoyance was making me nervous. He didn't stay there though, he walked around to say hi to his old friends and dance a bit.

Much later, Chris sat down next to me to catch up.

'Hey, you looking good these days, neh? How's life since Mobitech?' He was a bit tipsy and slurring ever so slightly.

'Thank you, Chris. Ag, it's been fine. Went back to study and stuff. You?' I kept a smile on my face and was cognisant of maintaining a good distance between myself and this man who wasn't my boyfriend.

'Didn't you have a baby with that other guy?'

'Yes, but we not together anymore.'

'What?' He didn't hear what I said. I leaned forward to repeat myself over the loud music.

'We not together anymore.' I was speaking into his ear. My bottom lip was on the verge of brushing it ever so lightly.

'You mos with Lyle now.' He turned to speak into my ear. I turned my head just in time to dodge a half full bottle of beer smashing into the wall next to us. I jumped up and Lyle reached over me, choking Chris. Another girl who was at our table grabbed my hand and led me to the bathrooms. I wasn't quite sure what was happening, but I just kept walking away from the scene.

'Yoh, that bra is really in love with you. I have never seen Lyle like that about a kin.' The compliments just kept on coming. I was both scared and flattered by what had happened. I had never been the girl in the midst of the commotion before and I felt important. In the spotlight. I left the bathroom and walked back to Lyle. Chris had left and I saw all the men around Lyle, speaking loudly about what they would have done to him if he had 'tried anything with Lyle's kin'.

I was definitely in trouble, but I stood next to him the whole night while he spoke about me as if I wasn't there. It felt confusing, but I enjoyed it. I felt important, enveloped in a relationship issue like a grown-up.

When we got home that night, he threatened to break up with me if I ever disrespected him like that again. I belonged at his side. If he was busy, I was to wait for him, without entertaining other brasse. His authority turned me on. I'd never made anyone jealous before.

But I still believed that his aggression was because of my actions and not because he was an aggressive person. If I was going to keep a man and keep him happy, I was to act a certain way.

In the next fight, however, he became aggressive with me, physically. It was also the first time I felt threatened by the thought that he was interested in other women. It all came flooding in at once, one thing after another.

We were sitting around the pool after a family lunch and his phone rang. He tilted the phone screen so that I couldn't really see the name and smiled at his phone before switching off the call.

'Who was that?' I wanted to sound casual.

'Hos, don't pla you with my phone.'

'What?' His reaction made me nervous. Had I misinterpreted the boundaries of our relationship? I never really knew anymore. He was jealous of my comings and goings, but always acted as if I had no authority to question his. It was a weird relationship tango that I never fully learned the moves to.

'Who was that, Lyle? Please don't lie.'

'It was my friend, What the fuck?' He escalated the conversation into an argument before I could even decide if I was angry. This was new.

'Please stop shouting.' We were right outside the door of my parents' house.

The house was built as a square court, with doors at different sections, all leading to the pool area where we stood. We could see into each door, which meant that people in those rooms could definitely see us.

'Jy, must I talk louder?' he threatened me, though my mind didn't register it as a threat at the time.

'Why are you being rude to me? I'm asking why you are talking to other women and hiding it.' I walked towards him, expecting him to be completely honest and show me who he had been chatting to. As I got to him, he switched it off. At the fucking power button. OFF-OFF.

'What the hell?' I shouted.

His eyes widened. The first time I would see them widen so intensely. He grabbed my arm and spun me around, before bear hugging me from behind. Head and face nestled in my neck, his grip around my body tightened, constricting my movement; it wasn't playful, although it was deliberately styled to look as if it was. As if we were dancing.

'Act lekker, act normal. Relax,' he whispered in my ear before I noticed that my family was watching. 'Don't let them notice we arguing.' He squeezed. I kept a straight face even though it was starting to hurt. I didn't want them to know what was going on, it wasn't their business.

'You making me cross. This is the second time you stress on my kop.'

'You not answering me ab—'

'Keep your bek,' he had a smile on his face. We looked like a couple sharing an affectionate embrace by the pool. I also smiled.

'You hurting me.' My air was running out. I didn't want them to know what he was doing and be upset with him . . . or be upset with me for being my usual difficult self.

'I'm not touching you.' He unhanded me, still keeping close so that I didn't lose my balance.

'If I didn't love you, I would have maarts. Don't dala this mad kak.'

I apologised for my indiscretion and didn't bring it up again.

'Hoe lyk it my hy willie meer vir jou hê nie?' Sometime in the week after, my mom mentioned nonchalantly in the kitchen that she thought he was going off me.

'What do you mean?' I was trying to remain calm, but that sentence had confirmed my fears.

124

'Hy hettie gelyk soes hy hier wil wiesi.' She was referring to lunch. He was on his phone the entire time. I had noticed that he didn't seem particularly excited to be there but brushed it off by laughing extra loud when he spoke to me.

'Hy het 'n ander goose,' she laughed. She was trying to be conversational, but telling me it looked like he had found some-one else was a shitty way to try and bond.

'We are fine, Mommy.'

'You stole him from Linda. Hy was tog eerste haar berk, toe steel jy vir hom. Hy willie vir jou gehad het nie. He never really wanted you.'

My heart sank into the pit of my stomach.

'Jy't geforce.'

That wasn't what happened.

I looked at my phone and changed my profile picture for the second time that morning, but he didn't message me until the next day.

'I have an interview tomorrow, ask your taani if I can use your car.' This was when things would start to change irreparably. And I would be lying if I said I didn't feel it all slipping away – I wasn't ready to admit to myself that he wasn't who I thought he had been. But the more he slipped away, the more my second chance did too. The idea of another man leaving me was so em-barrassing, especially because I was a single mommy.

He had already started to change his attitude toward my son.

When we were friends, he would play with Sidney for hours. But at the last family gathering he had embarrassed me so badly in front of everyone at the table. Sidney had said a word that Lyle always said. A slang word that I can't recall. But when he said it, I laughed and said, 'He gets that from you.'

Lyle looked at me, and through a smirk and snort said loudly,

125

'How, he isn't my laaitie.' Everyone at the table pretended they hadn't heard and I laughed, as if it hadn't stabbed me in the chest. But after that day, whenever we argued, he would add things like 'watch your laaitie, he's catching on kak'. It was always in front of others, like a warning shot for me to behave or he'd humiliate me.

Still, he was a good man with a temper. And a big sexual appetite. He hadn't hit me.

Not yet anyway.

# Chapter 9

# An escalation

When Lyle started his new Job, I was so excited that things were finally looking up for us. I began planning how things would be, without acknowledging the gaping holes in how things actually were.

He had changed his behaviour towards me, but I couldn't allow myself to let go of my plans. I was not going to lose the hope I felt. I was now in a desperate state, constantly trying to please him to win the initial affection back. If I just pleased him, he would remember how I used to make him feel. I craved the response I used to get from him, back when our relationship started. I had heard that after the initial romance relationships do go through a lull; I didn't think it would happen so suddenly.

This is where things get muddied.

I didn't realise it, but I was still in the thick of postnatal depression. In a way, I was relying on the happiness I had felt in the beginning of the relationship to be permanent. I could not bear a return to the emotional state I had been in before he came into my life. Really, at this stage the relationship should have been over: I should have moved forward, cut my losses. But going back felt terrifying. I was devastated at the idea of being without him and being wrong about another guy. I was gonna be so embarrassed.

Being with Lyle was changing me. I changed my ideals and moved my boundaries constantly to accommodate him. Of course, I noticed most of it after the fact, but in retrospect I realise that I did feel something was wrong. I was ignoring it, no matter how miserable and disappointing things were getting, to save face and save myself the pain of having to start over again.

I also think it's relevant to mention that Lyle knew that I was experiencing depression around my son and my situation. I had confided in him about my vulnerabilities and now I can see how he used that to figure out how far he could manipulate me and see just how desperate for him I was. He had started to push boundaries very soon in our relationship and did things that I wouldn't deem as appropriate now that I am in a healthier head-space. An example of this would be that I had spoken to him about how I didn't really enjoy sex as much as I had pretended to. I confided in him that I was mostly attracted to girls (when we were friends) and so from the moment we started sleeping together, he would attempt to have sex in the most inconvenient places. If I said no, or that I wasn't comfortable, he would ask me if it was because I didn't enjoy sex with him and if I wished that I was with a woman instead. It would make me feel obliged to give in to him, so that his feelings weren't hurt. The more I felt him drift away, the more sexually permitting I would be to make him enjoy being with me. He knew it and exploited the fact, asking me to do lewd things that made me want to cry, acting aloof until I gave in. Once he got his way I had a day or two of him being kind to me, until he wanted to try a new thing. I know it made him feel powerful – and it was sinister.

One evening I slept over at his house. He shared a room with his mother at the time and his bed was opposite hers. He had asked me if I was gonna 'give him' some, but I said I was uncomfortable at the idea of doing it in the same room as his mom. He said he understood, but the rest of the night he gave me a weird silent treatment. He wasn't full out ignoring me, but his responses to my attempts to talk were singsongy and minimal – and nonchalant. By the time we got into bed, I was exhausted by the emotional turmoil and I fell asleep almost immediately. I woke up to him thrusting into me, while his mom slept in the other bed. She woke up, but he didn't stop thrusting. I pretended to be asleep and tried to move away from him.

The next morning he pretended he had no idea what I was talking about.

On another occasion, he asked me to give him a blow job at my house, while my parents were home. I said no, but he said he always fantasised about getting a secret blow job and he wanted it to be from me. I was nervous about it, but obliged. He didn't tell me when my mom walked in midway. He made eye-contact with her and let me keep going till he came. Only afterwards he told me she had walked in and walked out again.

I thought he was lying, mostly because I didn't think anyone would have that little regard for another person. It didn't make sense to me that the man who loved me would want to demean me in front of others.

My mom mentioned to me a few days later that blow jobs could cause infections in the mouth. I pretended I had no idea what she was on about and walked away laughing. I cried that night. I couldn't stop the tears.

But none of these transgressions would hurt me as much as the revelation that he was cheating on me. In my opinion at the time, it was the most abusive act of all.

At the time that Lyle got a job at a company in Airport Industria, my parents had decided to move to a flat in Kenilworth. I was anxious about being so far away from Lyle, because I knew he had shown interest in another girl – a friend of my friend Caleb. Her name was Nadine and she was around six years younger than us. He denied it, though I saw they were chatting on BBM. But this job was going to change things for us, I knew it.

He asked me to ask my parents if he could use my car to get to work for the first month. I jumped at the idea – because surely he couldn't ghost me if he had my vehicle. I was obviously very stupid and very wrong. Writing this, I am cringing at my naivety. My logic, as I explained to my parents, was that he was taking this job to work towards our future. I was over the moon and unemployed.

My parents said yes and that day he left with my car. The smile on his face was so proud. I thought he would be grateful to me, but for the next three days I didn't see him. He said he was prepping for the job, but looking back I am not sure what that meant. It wasn't necessarily skilled or educated labour, that he would need to brush up his skills for. Everything was done onsite, so the only prep would be to pack one's lunch the night before.

He did come see me off the day my family and I moved: he was an hour late, but I waited for him in front of the empty house. Sidney went to the flat with my parents so long and I stayed behind with my dad's car. I was so sad about leaving. I would be so far from him now, but I took solace in knowing that he was building our future. We would live together soon.

He came to the house smelling of weed and alcohol. He kissed me and said he was enjoying his new job and that he had been so busy that he was too tired to chat in the evenings. He assured me that this was the company he would work for the rest of his life. He spoke excitedly of the growth opportunities and how he

130

would buy a house in five years. But something felt off. I assumed it was my insecurities.

'I have to go now. I wanna drive before it gets dark.' I leaned in to kiss him. He didn't lean in himself, but allowed the kiss.

'Sorry, I'm moeg, man,' he smiled.

'Are you gonna drive behind me and come see the flat?'

'Naai, I don't smaak, man. Then it's a mission to get home tonight.'

'But you have my car?' Why wouldn't he want to make sure I got there safely or see where I was staying?

'Oh ja. You know what I mean, man. And don't keep the car over my kop, man. You can hou it if you gonna be like that. I'll just make another plan for work.'

'No, I didn't mean it like that.' I went down the outside stairs to lock up the back doors. When I got to the bottom, I hadn't noticed that he had followed me down. I felt nervous about where the conversation was going. If he didn't have my car, I had no excuse to message him first. It was reason for him to reply to me.

'So there's other mense gonna move in here you say?' He walked past me into the house.

'Apparently.'

'Yoh, your ou is dom to let people fok up so 'n joint. What if they mess it up? Yoh. And I thought we inherit it when he dies?' He laughed so loudly that it echoed. I had never heard the house echo before. I felt my eyes tear up, an infrequent sensation at that time of my life. Tears were pathetic. I was kind of excited that I was crying, so that he could comfort me. He didn't.

'And now, why you sad?'

I immediately felt sheepish.

'Kak mad,' he said.

'I'm not man, it's just heavy.'

131

'Come here baby, man.' He pulled me by the pants pocket. I leaned in for a hug, but that wasn't what his body was doing.

He pulled my pants down and grabbed me by the waist. When he kissed my lips, I didn't recognise what he felt like.

'No man,' I was laughing as I said it.

'What you mean no? We alone here.'

'I have to drive, it's late and Sidney is with my mommy.'

'Isn't he always with your mommy?' He didn't smile when he said that. He was still holding me with light force. I wanted to loosen myself from his grip, but I didn't want him to be angry. I didn't feel comfortable standing undressed in the lounge. The walls were mostly glass doors and it didn't feel like home now that it was empty. All that was left was a mat. We were standing on it.

'Come man, I had a long day at work,' he said seductively into my neck. I didn't feel seduced, but I felt pressured to give him myself as a reward. I didn't want to be a party pooper. I stood still for a few seconds, thinking. He put more pressure into his grip.

He rolled his eyes.

'Never mind. I wanted this to be romantic, like you are kind of leaving me here in Strandfontein.'

He walked away and I felt so disappointed that I had spoiled his gesture.

'No wait,' I called him. He turned around to look at me and smiled.

He came back to the mat without speaking and took off my clothes. We had sex on the floor. I didn't notice until the end that I was the only one undressed.

'You must go, it's getting late,' he said almost simultaneously with cumming. I wanted to cuddle, but the mat had short, rough bristles. He must not have been comfortable.

132

I locked up and we walked back to the cars. He kissed me and got into my car and drove off. I watched him leave. I felt uneasy about how he had said goodbye. This wasn't how I had pictured the day. But I knew he was in a hurry to get home and shower and sleep. He was a man with a job and that needed to be respected.

Before making my way home, I thought to go pop in at Caleb's place in Strandfontein. Caleb was my childhood friend. Lyle and I frequented his house and he and his boyfriend always welcomed us for sleepovers and a few puffs of dagga. But when I arrived, my car was parked outside. Lyle was there.

I drove past.

I told myself that he was probably just saying hi or picking something up. I couldn't imagine how crazy I'd look if I also stopped there now. I just went home.

In the weeks that followed, Lyle didn't visit me much. He said he was working and for the most part he was – but even on his off days he would only message me once or twice, between naps.

I would be in a constant state of waiting. Being the woman in the relationship took power out of my hands. It was like that for most relationships at the time. Men were to initiate. Men were to propose. Men were to lead. Even now, as I write this in 2020, this is true. Women spend decades in relationships, waiting for the man-child they are dating to propose. Even independent, virtually perfect women who have a life plan and goals and shit just stay in limbo, with bated breath. And men are allowed to be emotionless and inactive, as if their gender is born clueless. A lovely scapegoat. A biological excuse for having zero accountability, even about the feelings of your significant other. Women are forced to jump through hoops and pretend to be needier than they really are to extract even a drop of reaction from these fucking Dementors. And the reward? He will maybe marry you and then make you his official slave, before God and Facebook (and the law and stuff). We drive ourselves crazy faking pregnancies, miscarriages and suicidal behaviour, just to reassure ourselves that they do care about us – even if it's only in the brief amount of time they are conscious between their PlayStation games. Like the meme lords say, 'if he pauses his game to respond to you – it isn't common decency – it's real love'.

But this wasn't even like that. This relationship was darker.

One day, Caleb sent me a BBM.

'Hey friend, you doing okay in the new place?'

I wasn't.

'When did you and Lyle break up?'

'What do you mean?' I used positive emojis to hide my horror at the question. My mind had already catapulted back into its Crescent Clinic form.

'He said you broke up, but you let him use your car?' My heart ballooned.

'He is bymekaar with Nadine.'

I was too embarrassed to say that we hadn't broken up. I was shaking as I typed, 'yes, we broke up LOL'. It felt like I was fucking seizing. I knew he had liked Nadine all along. This whore 18-year-old. Caleb's baby sister's friend who had swaaid her gatjie 'n bietjie too wild when the big boys were lamming and smoking at Caleb's house. Her confidence really worked on my poes; it was an affront to the older kinnes who already had laaities. She had that new car smell that men who were in long-term relationships liked. After years of being the young kin who was 'bets to chise your berk', I was now the old girlfriend who had a laaitie. I hadn't even noticed the transition until that very moment.

As it turns out, Lyle had been visiting her on the nights that he had said he was sleeping. My car had been parked outside of her home quite a few times before Caleb had noticed. In the unravelling, it was revealed that on the three occasions he had visited me in the weeks leading up to Caleb telling me everything, he had only come because she hadn't wanted to have sex on those particular days and I never declined. At least I think I didn't. I don't remember having a choice.

That night, shaking and nauseous, I made my way to Caleb's house. I remember it in slow motion for some reason. Recalling the exact emotions as I parked behind my own car, just knowing that they were both in there, still infuriates me almost a decade later. I was so bitter, enraged. My energy was deadly. I was ready to kill Nadine. I wanted to sink my nails into her skin. I wanted my fingernails to pull down the bottom lids of her eyes and tear the flesh off her face like putty.

I walked in, past Caleb, straight into the back room. It smelled of dagga and something musty that I couldn't pinpoint. The two of them sat with a few others around a round, unvarnished wooden table, playing UNO. Just casually playing UNO while they were deceiving me.

Lyle stood up and grabbed my arm to walk me out the room. His eyes were wide.

'Hello baby, come we talk in the other room.' He tugged my elbow.

But I broke free and pushed past him to Nadine. She had tried to leave, but I blocked the doorway. He stood against the wall, creating a barrier between her and me. At the time, I thought it was to protect her, but now I know it was to stop her from telling me anything.

'How can you do this to us? I even gave you my car to use to build our life!' The whole room stared at me.

135

'Your taani gave me your car,' he laughed and signaled the ouens with his eyes, as if to say, 'Check this kin going on'.

'What?' It didn't make sense that he would say something that vapid. I must have misunderstood. Technically he wasn't wrong.

'Jy maak 'n scene, Shana . . .' He raised his voice.

'Of course I am making a fucking scene. You told her we were broken up?'

'Are yous still together?'

She spoke out of turn. I wanted to pull her whore throat out.

'Keep your bek. How can you choose this sleg, worthless poes over me? She's a vark laaitie. Look at her, sies.' I was spewing fucking venom. I could feel it spilling out from my stomach. I felt relieved of it with every word I released at them.

I spent some more time berating her. In my head, she was younger than me and she was the one who was wrong. She had no reason to defend herself.

'You poes, you jintoe,' she shouted at me and grabbed a spade that was leaned against the wall. She lifted it to hit me and Lyle grabbed her. Caleb stood between us.

'Hit me, jou naai.' I didn't give her the chance. I put all ten of my fingers deep into her hair and gripped tight. I felt the hairs rip from her head. They were so fragile. I pulled her by her hair from the room. Her screams gave me so much pleasure.

We moved through the house. People grabbed my hands, trying to pry her loose but I was going to kill her in the road. The rage had possessed me. She had committed the ultimate sin. She was trying to steal my man.

Lyle walked behind us the whole way. I didn't look at his face. I saw his legs. Their gait was slow, casual.

I let go of her hair in the road. She was crying like a child. I considered how she only wanted to be a child when it was convenient.

136

'You a jintoe! He don't want you,' she tjunked loudly.

Everyone was just standing around. Not in a circle, but far away, like they didn't want to be part of any of it. Lyle stood next to me. She kept her eyes on him.

'How can you leave me for someone whose fucking brain can only come up calling me a jintoe?' It didn't even make sense. She was stealing MY boyfriend. Fucking Neanderthal bitch.

I grabbed her again. She grabbed me. We held each other, suspended in time in the middle of the goddamn street. Both screaming. I don't know how much time passed, but when we looked up, Lyle was far down the road, walking home.

I let go of her. She fell into Caleb's arms. I ran up the road.

'Yes, your poes, go home. I fucking hate you!' I screamed past the massive monument that stood at the end of Gazala Crescent.

I reached a bench and sat down. I felt Caleb's hand on my shoulder. We sat down on the bench and I collapsed into his lap. My head on his knees. I sobbed so hard my stomach and chest pained.

'Where's Nadine?'

'In the house. You hurt her, Shana. Her hair is out.'

We laughed.

'Yoh, Lyle is a poes. He told her you guys broke up weeks ago.'

'We didn't, Caleb. Yoh. I knew he smaaked her. That other night when we were all here I saw how he was acting with her.'

'Me too,' Caleb stroked my head.

Lyle approached us. I sat up. Caleb got up and walked back home and Lyle sat down. He was smiling.

'I never told that kin nothing, she is lying to you. We just smoked together after work.'

'Why couldn't you smoke with Caleb?' I really wanted to believe him.

137

'Caleb don't always have. She koppeld from her berk.'

I started to feel sheepish. Of course he wasn't cheating on me. I calmed down. My stomach unknotted a bit. He held me.

'You mos started a new job, ow die girl!' he laughed.

'Yeah. It's lekker. I start on Monday.'

'What is the pay?' He stuck out his tongue and raised his eyebrows.

'R8000.'

'Yoh. Baller money! Our dream is coming true, baby.' He poked my side. I couldn't help but smile.

'Come we go. This mense gran to make kak. I wanted to wys you they talk a klom kak about you, but they your friends, sien jy?'

'What do they say?' Why was he telling me they had been talking kak about me? The knot tightened again.

'Naai, don't still worry. It's just heavy, sien jy? This mense is not your friends.'

We went back to Caleb's house and fetched my cars. We left and I went to Lyle's house. When we got there, we stood outside, against the cars. He held me around my waist and kissed me. A man I didn't recognise walked up to us and took his hand.

'Aweh, is die jou aap?' he pointed to his own nipples, one by one. I didn't really appreciate being called a monkey, but at least he seemed to know I was Lyle's woman.

'Ja, die man lyk gooooodt. Die is my motchie.'

'Waars Nadine, dan? Roeki vanandie?' I noticed he assumed Lyle would be smoking with Nadine.

'Nah, my kin klap haar dan nou net, hier agter in Trafalgar.'

'Wet?' This man was so impressed at the story of how I'd just hit Nadine.

'Nadine trip?' the stranger continued, laughing as if he had known me for years and found it amusing that I had behaved out of character.

138

'Naai my girl kan fight,' Lyle laughed. He was proud. I felt proud that he was proud. I had showed him not to fuck with me.

We kept dating after that night. I purposefully blocked the Nadine debacle from my mind although I had confirmation that he and she were in fact a thing behind my back. I decided I couldn't bear the thought of losing him, so I would accept the affair – like a big girl. I was angrier with her for the betrayal than with him. He was always a hypersexual person. He was a man and she was willing – of course he was gonna dala.

I started to create email addresses to email Nadine from. I sent pages and pages of emails detailing how he chose me and how she was dirt and beneath me. I threatened to tell her boy-friend that she let him fuck her and that I knew they had fucked. I had seen the messages on his phone.

The emails went on for longer than I am proud of. If I went a day without harassing her, I would get the urge to message her. Then, in the first few hours after ejaculating emails to this woman/child, I would wait, just staring at my phone. I kept imag-ining her sending me a message, revealing what really happened.

She never replied. Only once, to tell me that she was going to the police. She never did.

For the next few months, Lyle was back to being the man he had been when we were friends. We chatted every day and seemed to be finding a real rhythm in our relationship. We both worked and made time to chat between our lunchtimes and, with our strong budget, we did things on weekends. But while the relationship was booming, my life at home was not.

My parents expected me to get home from work and spend time with my kid. It felt like a punishment.

I had initially thought that having a happy relationship would make me happier in all aspects of my life, but I still saw Sidney

139

as a burden, an obstacle. I couldn't just go on dates or do any-thing on a whim like a young woman of my age should have been able to. Of course, it wasn't Sidney's fault, but he was a manifes-tation of my stupidity and I couldn't stand being near him.

I was also so resentful that Hashiem was off scot-free while I was forever bound. Lyle was visibly annoyed on the days I said I had to be home with Sidney. It meant he would need to choose between going out and having a good time, or being with his kin and her laaitie. The truth was that he didn't need to be punished for my irresponsibility – it was unfair on him. And it was making kak for me with him, because I could feel his disinterest loom-ing again. Between the anger and the inconvenience of being trapped and the dangerous thoughts I started to have about my child who was now nearly two, I made the decision to leave. One day, I packed my bag and told him I was moving out of my mom's house. I had some money and was going to find my own place. I asked if he would help me find one. I wasn't actually sure what to do. I assumed I could just approach someone who was renting on Gumtree and pay the rent and that would be it.

I walked to the main street near my parents' apartment. Lyle was there, waiting. I had one backpack. He kissed me and sig-nalled a taxi. I saw Sidney at the apartment window, looking out at me, waving. I pretended I didn't see him and climbed in.

When we got to the City Centre, Lyle immediately pulled rank on me. He was the street-smart one. I had been to town many times, but he said that I didn't know what other ouens were think-ing, so I allowed him to lead. He chose our route to the Company Gardens. He told me to buy a few beers and we sat on a bench near a family of ducks. I had been to that same bench many times. I'd been there the first time I saw the Klopse in town with my Heights friends as a teen and I'd walked through there as a student journalist, on my way to see my first court case. And now, I sat there as a grown-up, illegally drinking a beer I didn't want to drink, to impress a man who only loved me sometimes.

Between moments of thinking that I should call my mom, I scrolled through Gumtree. I couldn't help thinking that I had never been out as an adult without having a kid at home. I had never known freedom and I am convinced my body was rejecting it.

'So, what's the next move?' he sat, manspread next to me. He took up two thirds of the bench. The perfect metaphor.

'What do you mean? I need to find a place. I wanna rent somewhere.'

'You mos the girl with the money,' he took a sip.

For context, he had quit his job again. Wasn't the right fit for him. He was going to find something closer to home and easier to travel to. My dad asked for my car back and that meant that he would have to take a bus and a taxi to work, so he resigned. He hadn't even discussed it with me. He just decided to nip our dream, or at the very least detour away from it. Luckily, I was working and in a position to cover my own rent until he found another job –then maybe he could move in after a while. At least, that's what I assumed he would do. But he had other ideas.

Now, in the Gardens, it was getting late. It would be night soon and I still hadn't found a place to live, or even to sleep that evening.

'Come, we eat somewhere?' He spoke my language. We ended up in Kloof street at the Fat Cactus opposite City Varsity. Margarita litres at Happy Hour will fuck you up. We walked to a bank after paying and I drew a few thousand rand. Back to Fat Cactus. It was a lekker vibe.

We spoke to the other people from the surrounding tables.

Lyle had a way of gravitating people towards a party. He made friends with an older white woman and left me alone at the table for a bit to chat to her. He returned to me, excited.

'I sorted our accommodation.' He was proud of himself.

I was immediately skeptical.

'Where are we gonna sleep?'

'In Pinelands. That lady said we can sleep in her spare room.'

It didn't feel right at all.

'Why would she say that?' I was very tipsy.

'Cos I'm reg.' He laughed out loud.

I felt embarrassed, but the music was loud too. The vibe was wild and erratic.

'Come man, she said her husband said it's irie.'

'It's what?'

'Just come, they leaving now. She gave me the address. I said we still gonna grab something to eat, then we can go to her house afterwards.'

'How?

'You can mos pay for a taxi?'

'I don't wanna go to a stranger's . . .'

'Yoh, you permy make kak man – you always making trouble,' he shouted at me. No one looked. He lowered his voice. 'Whenever I have a solution you don't take it, but you complain I don't do manly things. I do manly things for you, Shana, start treating me like a man.'

I both knew and had no idea what that meant.

I looked over to the lady's table. She and a group of white people and one Indian lady sat there, drinking and laughing. The man beside her, who turned out to be her husband, wasn't laughing though. He looked upset with her, as she sat next to him pretending to smile. I can spot a pretend smile from tables away.

They left and Lyle called a cab. I had never been in a cab before. From Kloof to Pinelands was R700.

'Stop by Kentucky, my bru,' he asked the driver. We went
through the drive-through at the KFC in Observatory.

'You also want something? My kin will buy it.'

I still hadn't spoken since greeting the cab driver. I was half
asleep. Lyle took my purse and bought himself and the driver a
meal. It was an extra R50 to add a stop to the trip. By the time
we got to Pinelands I was R1200 down, for one car ride. I was so
tired, I just wanted to sleep. I couldn't party anymore.

'Who are you?' the Indian woman who opened the door to the
Pinelands home repeated. The house was large and beautiful, but
by no means the mansion Lyle had promised. 'Barbara invited
us. From Fat Cactus,' he said.

She looked deadpan. Past a pillar, we could see everyone in
the entertainment area. A bricked, indoor braai and couch separated from the main house by a sliding door. Rich people things.
It was evident that the very few guests were all close friends and
no one had been onboard with us joining them. But Lyle didn't
seem to read the room, or care enough about the atmosphere to
bow out gracefully. I stood there, uneasy and embarrassed.

The woman from the restaurant pushed past the door lady and
welcomed us anyway. She was quite drunk.

'Barbara,' her husband called, in a short, aggressive burst. She
excused herself and swayed to the kitchen. We stood in the
entrance. The Indian lady still stood there too, just watching us.

Barbara returned.

'You guys can sleep upstairs.'

The Indian lady led us upstairs, but kept looking back at us as
we walked. She took us to the spare room. Lyle took out a bottle
of spirits that we had bought earlier. It was opened, but still about

three-quarters full. I felt embarrassed that we could only offer used beverages. He was proud enough though, and we dropped our bags and went down to the party.

I sat by the fire and Lyle immediately started dancing, pouring a drink. He showed the bottle to everyone, holding it in the air, pumping it up and down to the beat.

'We brought 'n ietsie,' he laughed.

No one responded. The party had died. I knew why, though. I had been on the other side of this situation before, when Coloured 'lesser than' people entered my college friends' parties. I could suddenly smell my armpits. I had been drinking in the sun for most of the afternoon and had all my clothes in a Karrimor. I had never been more self-aware than that moment. I was the rough element and these people were wary of me. I wanted to speak of my degree and my journalism career. But I wouldn't even know how to begin socialising or slipping it in there. The way they were looking at Lyle also made me nervous. I had seen loads of men look at him that way before and it always ended in a fight. He rubbed other men up the wrong way.

'I party with any mense, sien jy?' he spoke to the men, oblivious that he was outclassed. I was very embarrassed by him. But I had already decided he was my man, so I would have to bite through it. I didn't even consider that I didn't have to be with him.

'Naai, yous then aren't paaaartying.' He really emphasised the PAAAAAA part to sound as gangster as possible. 'Me and wifey are ma gonna go sleep,' he said, winking at me and sticking out his tongue.

I know he was waiting for them to laugh. But he was unfamiliar with this calibre of person. I felt stuck on the median. I laughed to make him not look so stupid.

We walked up the stairs, the Indian lady behind us.

144

'Unfortunately, I've been asked to tell you guys to leave,' she said, as we got to the room.

'What?' I had never been the element that needed to leave before. I felt as if my own kind of coconut wasn't recognising me.

'Barbara said we can. Call her, it's her joint.' Lyle's voice sounded aggressive.

'Excuse me . . .' She raised her voice.

I got nervous, took my bag and cleaned up my accent. 'It's okay, we will leave.' It felt liberating to take charge.

'Thank you for understanding and co-operating.'

'Can I first use the restroom please, then we will leave?' I dunno why the fuck I suddenly had the word 'restroom' in my vocabulary.

She paused and looked me up and down. 'Sure.' She rolled her eyes and walked down the stairs.

'You can come with me so long,' she told Lyle.

'Ja, let me get my bag.'

I went into the guest toilet exhausted, confused. I looked around the gorgeous bathroom. I admired the bath. The woman had so many products and gadgets. The lighting even had settings. It was both dim and romantic, a natural aesthetic. I wanted my own place with my own bathroom. She used the same beauty products as my sister.

I peed and a defiant, indignant part of my psyche made me take my time. I wiped and didn't flush yet. I just wanted a few more moments of being in a quiet, comfortable space. I was accustomed to this, but now I watched from the outside every time I met up with an old friend, or entered a boutique store, or spoke to an educated person and then had to say that I had had a baby. Or when people I knew met my boyfriend and he didn't act like us. I wanted to pretend, just for a little bit longer that I didn't have to go outside into the cold, with nowhere to sleep.

I washed my hands and my face and looked in the mirror. In the reflection, I saw Barbara's GHD flatiron on the shelf next to the bath. I felt such intense jealousy. It was the new one too. The one that can be charged and used without the lead. This one allowed you to fry your hair from never-before-seen angles. I sighed deeply. 'One day', I thought. Then, in a wave of jealous rage, I grabbed it and the cable and slipped it into my bag. I flushed before I could reconsider. I exited the bathroom and Indian lady was standing at the top of the stairs, so that she could be there when I came out and could see Lyle at the foot of the stairs at the same time.

She walked us out into the cold.

She closed the door before my back foot was on the pavement.

'Run,' I told Lyle.

He didn't ask any questions and we ran. With each step, I felt regret. I wasn't a thief, what was I doing?

We finally stopped at a parking lot, outside of some sort of country club. We landed on the grass and burst out laughing. I hadn't seen him laugh this hard since we were friends.

'Why we running?' he laughed.

'I stole something,' I waited to be reprimanded.

'Don't talk kak. What did you take?' He kept giggling.

'I took that naai's GHD.' I felt so liberated.

'Lies! Show me.'

I opened the bag and pulled it out a little. Lyle's eyes lit up. He looked at me in adoration.

'Naai een ding, klas,' he added a hand gesture to emphasise the savageness of my actions. 'You a mal naai!' It was a compliment. 'Die is klom geld.'

The last time he had been this proud of me, I had fought Nadine. I was in a different world, but at least I was winning.

'What kyn there upstairs?' Lyle asked a car guard lady who had come our way on her rounds. Upon further inspection, she was a homeless woman wearing a green reflector jacket. She sat down by us and pointed to the bottle we were finishing.

'Gee bietjie daar, man.' She wanted some, but we didn't have cups. The idea of having a bergie put her mouth on the same thing as I put mine on was sobering. Another metaphor I blocked out. At the time engrained classism had turned me into a piece of shit.

Lyle didn't hesitate to hand her the bottle. She drank slow and deep.

It is very important to tell you that I no longer hold the classist, assholist views I did as a young woman. I do want to give you an accurate depiction of my mindset at the time. I was a trash bag, raised by a trash bag world.

'Aaaah,' she smiled. Lyle was impressed. Her drinking skills were impeding my winning streak. This was my night. I took the bottle and tried my best to ignore the burn, but took solace in the fact that it was neutralising the homeless saliva.

They didn't even look at me. There was no way I was doing it again, not even for the clout. The vomit crept up my throat and sat in wait. I kept my mouth shut.

'A cricket club reunion paaarty of iets.' She pointed to the two-story building.

'We go in?' He looked excited.

'It's probably an invite-only move,' I code-switched again. This time downward. 'Jy, their poes, man. They don't wys me.'

It felt wrong walking in behind him. The team was upstairs, drinking. There were a few women, young ones. Everyone turned

147

to look at us. Everyone was white. There was a token black kid with them, who met us at the door.

'Hey bru, this is a private gig, my china.' He was friendly, but his body language was protective.

I waited for Lyle to react. I just stood there, stinky and nervous. I smiled at everyone, wildly underdressed for the occasion.

'Okay, let's leave then. We know what is going on here.'

'What do you mean, bru?' Token asked.

'Nah. It's cool bru,' Lyle motioned for me. The alcohol must have kicked in with full potency, because the next thing I remember we were down in the parking lot again and the guys from the party were leaving. Lyle was arguing with someone. The guy tried to get in his car and drive away, but Lyle grabbed his rear-view mirror and then smashed the windscreen, hitting it with a flat hand.

The guy stopped the car and climbed out, but again the details are blurry. The next thing I knew, we were sitting on the grass with the homeless lady.

'Yoh, I smashed that man's windscreen with my bare hand my bru. I am kak strong,' Lyle sat back, leaning onto his flat palms. His chest was puffed out a little too far forward for the position to be comfortable. 'Naai, I'm a gees!' he laughed loudly again.

'Do we still have kroon left?' he asked me.

'Yes, I do.' I was saving it for a place to stay.

'Now what is your plan for us for the night? It's getting late. I'm moeg.'

'Daar's 'n shelter, lanks die stasie.'

Lyle was very excited by the revelation that there was a shelter at the station. I felt my stomach make a final knot. I convulsed and vomit catapulted from every hole in my face.

'Naaaaaai man!' He and Homeless laughed at me. I couldn't

148

help but let it out. As humiliating as it was, it was so freeing to expel.

They laughed at me. He leaned into her midsection as they laughed. They looked like a team. I lay back to feel the cold air on my face. It had been quite a clean execution, though. My face was only a little wet around the orifices. My sleeve sorted that out.

'Come, it's getting late.' Lyle put his bag on his back. I stood up and followed him over the field and past a few shops to the station. After 15 minutes we arrived at a hostel of sorts. There was a security guard outside, but the place looked uninhabited. It had a kitchen and a watching area but nothing else.

I sat on the couch under the cheap fluorescent lights of the common room. The TV played silently on e.tv.

'We go smoke a entjie,' Lyle motioned me to the door.

'No, it's cold. My feet are paining.' I pointed. I wasn't used to walking this much.

'Forgot you mos not a trot manskap. Spoilt, mos,' he laughed at me. 'This is life when your daddy can't buy you a car.' He stood up and stretched.

'Come, you not gonna sit here alone, I don't trust this manne,' he nodded his head to security. There were now two of them at the door.

'I don't trust black brasse, they gran dik kinnes.'

I laughed. I got up and got my Adidas hoodie from my bag. I zipped up and followed. He walked off the stoep onto the pavement and sat down, feet in the road. I sat next to him. I was worried that I was leaving my bags in a strange place, alone. My GHD was in there.

And then, as he handed me my skyf, something descended upon me. Something persuasive. Something very much linked to my OCD.

'Why did you have sex with Nadine?' I blurted out. 'Please tell me why?'

'Not this kak again, Shana.' He stood up to walk back in. I got up behind him and showed him. I was suddenly livid. Maybe it was the exhaustion, maybe it was the constant berating even though he should have been grovelling. But I hit him on his arm. He turned around and without even pausing to look at me, he smacked me across the face.

This was the first time he had ever hit me. This was the first time a man had hit me.

I buckled. He raised his massive windscreen-breaking hand even higher and smacked me again. And again. And again.

When I fell to the ground, I thought he would stop. He had proven his point. My mom usually stopped when I fell. He had to have empathy for me. He loved me.

Lyle grabbed the hood of my Adidas hoodie and pulled at it so hard that I heard the fabric rip. He dragged me down the road as I struggled to breathe – the top acting as a noose, while the zip cut into my chin. I still have the mark.

'Jy slaanie vir my nie, Shana – don't you hit me. Daai issie jou werkie, hoor jy?' He was shouting at me in Afrikaans, telling me it wasn't my job to discipline him, but he wasn't even Afrikaans. He was speaking as if there was an audience. It turns out there was, he just didn't know it.

He threw me across the street and hit me again.

He stopped. I turned around and tried to focus my eyes as best I could, to see the two security guards holding him by the arms. He struggled to get free.

They hit him simultaneously. He wasn't strong enough to fight two men.

Are you okay? the one asked me.

Lyle threw expletives and racial slurs as he swung his arms in desperation. They didn't relent.

He screamed like a girl.

'Baby! They killing me. Help me,' he shouted at me. 'They killing me, call the cops.'

I ran to them and held him. 'Leave my boyfriend, please. Leave him,' I screamed. I was in tears.

'Please, I am gonna call the cops. Please.' They stared at me, confused. They stopped hitting Lyle and said something in isiXhosa that I can only assume was 'look at this stupid bitch'. Rightfully so.

He held onto me as I went to get our bags. We walked away from the hostel. My mind hadn't fully grasped what had happened, or what was happening.

'You didn't have to bring up Nadine. Look how you made kak now.' He dialed his pa's number.

When we got picked up, I sat in silence while he made casual conversation with his grandpa. I climbed into bed and slept off the night.

The next day, I went to check out a place to stay in Westlake. I paid the deposit and watched, powerless, as Lyle packed a bag and came with me to the new place. I didn't invite him. I actually hadn't spoken to him since the night before.

When we got there, his pa left and he and I stood there, in the middle of the separate entrance.

'How are you gonna get home? You pa left,' I mumbled through swollen lips.

'What? My kin isn't gonna live alone, where am I gonna allow that?'

I remember just staring at him, defeated, confused. I was scared at the way the relationship was changing ever so quickly.

'What do you wanna dala here?'

'You hit me, Lyle,' I said. I didn't think I needed to elaborate on why I wasn't exactly keen to be near him.

'Talk kak. I never hit a kin before,' he said. I actually questioned myself for a second. I wondered if I had misinterpreted the situation or at least the severity.

'I was gesuip, you know, completely out of it, Shana,' he continued.

He unpacked his clothes into a drawer.

# Chapter 10

# Bek/fist in bed

I would like to take a break for a second and tell you a story about my extended family and, in particular, the story of my Aunty Brenda. Aunty Brenda was the first single mom I knew. I think she may have been the only one I ever encountered before my teens.

For years, Brenda and her son were alone. I couldn't wrap my head around how she had a child, but didn't have a husband. Just as confusing was the question of why my cousin Esra lived with my grandparents in the main house without her mom, who was married to a man who wasn't her father. Ezra's sisters grew up with her mother and their father. But he didn't want to have another man's child under his roof, in his wallet. My aunty would visit her daughter at my grandma's house, and bring her clothes and other things. At family functions at my grandmother's house, Esra would watch her mother arrive with her new family. It was my aunt's own fault for having children before marriage, though. Her husband wasn't expected to support her stupid indiscretion. Issie sy kindtie – not his child. At the time, a reasonable attitude (apparently it still is).

Regardless, Brenda was the only one of my dad's sisters who still lived at home and they treated her like a child, because she wasn't married. It was hard for me to respect her, because I wasn't forced to; not like I was made to revere my other, wed aunties. Even the one who had swapped out her illegitimate child for a man who openly treated her like garbage.

It is important to say that my father's brothers received respect regardless of how they behaved.

Two of my uncles did hard drugs, two were cheaters who fathered several children behind their wife's back. One couldn't keep a job and one was just fine. Two of them asked me for money every time they saw me, and this continued into my adulthood. If the request wasn't for money, it was for entjies.

'Shana, het jy nie 'n twee rand vir jou pa se broer nie?' My uncle always spoke of himself in the third person when loafing from me. It was a weird way of reminding me that even though he was asking me for something, I was still the child.

Aunty Brenda was a gorgeous, slender woman – she had beautiful straight hair and I always appreciated how friendly she was compared to my father's other sisters. But I suppose that the years of enduring her singleton, tainted woman status had whittled her down because she eventually wed a family friend who had no job and no money. Nothing besides a penis and willingness to be a husband. His name was Uncle Chinky.

Uncle Chinky, as I had learned to know him, was a charismatic, friendly man. I knew him from before their courtship. He was one of the uncles who helped my daddy build our house in Pelican Heights from the foundation up. As a six-year-old, I used to run through the dusty building while the men worked.

While the men built my father's dream house, my mom would be in the bottom of the house preparing tea and sandwiches, my sister somewhere else. I would run through a very sandy, undeveloped Pelican Heights. For most of the day I was unattended. The bushes were thick and enticing when I was a child. I stayed out the way of the men who were working, but I knew them all as my uncles. I found out many years later that I wasn't related to most of them; they were just men who had grown up at my father's childhood home. It was customary for people of colour to unofficially adopt other people's kids. Uncle Chinky was one of these random people, but he always made time to listen to my stories. I haven't seen him in over 20 years and I can still remember how he made me feel. He was kind. He didn't make fun of me for being sturvy like the rest of my dad's family did.

Apparently at this time he pursued Aunty Brenda and she had fallen for his charm, as I would say the rest of us did. By the late 90s when my father's house was complete, he and Aunty Brenda had gotten married. But there were a few things that didn't seem quite right for me.

Firstly, he didn't take her from her father's home. Instead, he moved into the separate entrance she already occupied behind my ma's house. He merely took up more space in her already cramped life. He didn't work anymore and he was always a little bit drunk whenever we would visit. He was still so kind to me though, interested in how I was doing. It didn't take long before the family started to whisper of his shenanigans.

When the rumours of his indiscretions touched my baby ears, I couldn't picture him losing his temper.

I couldn't quite make the connection between the uncle who was always the life of the party and the man they said was hitting his wife. The more refined women would always blame the 'type' my aunty was for her bad luck in marriage.

'Wat het sy gemaak,' is still a favourite line of the churchly old aunties I encounter against my will to this day. The answer: she must have provoked him, of course. It is the rationalisation, the equaliser whenever a man violates a woman's boundaries.

I digress; one evening my family hired a hall in Retreat for

155

some or other cousin's 21st celebration and Brenda and Chinky were there. Johnny and his new half-sister sat with them. The family looked well. But as at most Coloured functions, the darker it got, the longer the trips to the 'cars with the dop' in the parking lot. At around 10pm that night, Uncle Chinky entered the venue positively pickled.

People turned to look at him, falling around, but no one intervened.

Brenda walked outside, embarrassed. He followed. I didn't. But the commotion and screaming that was audible from my seat was enough of an indication of what had transpired. The women in my family rushed Brenda to the public toilets that lined the entrance. I didn't want to seem too invested, but slowly walked towards the bathroom under the guise of needing to pee. I was still too young to inquire. I smiled and went into the stall.

'Hy's weer dik gesuip,' Captain Obvious comforted her by pointing out her man was drunk when he hit her.

'Hy't vir haar hardt geklap, die vark.'

The men did nothing. The women could merely drag her to the safety of the heterosexual bathroom walls.

I took lekker long in the stall. They all stood around her and comforted her. When I exited, a whole group was hovering over her, like flies around someone's life falling to shit. Some sat on the counters around the basin, against the mirror. The two senior flies each held her with one arm, her in the middle, staring at the ground. She looked contemplative and at the same time, blank. Numb. Exhausted.

The next time we visited my ma, months later, Chinky was still Brenda's husband. A few years later, I was a teen already, my father was called to remove him from the property. I went with him that day.

When we got there, Chinky was outside in the yard. My father's sisters were all there too. They had called on him to sort out the situation. As the oldest brother, he had a duty to protect his family. My dad instructed me to stay in the main house and he went to the yard unarmed. Looking back, that was a dangerous move, but my dad held superhero stature in my mind. He still does.

'Jy kan nog nooit my suster soe slattie, Chinky,' I only caught the arse end of the conversation, my father telling him not to hit his sister. I realised that if I stood in the back room of the house, I could see into the yard.

'Vat jou goed en fokkof.' Now he was telling him to leave.

'Naai man, Toks. Jy wiet issie ekkie – it's her fault, not mine. Sy slaap rond ...'

My father ignored the claim that she'd been sleeping round. 'Chinky, vat jou goed en fokof. Jy kommie weer op my ma-hulle se property nie. En jy,' he addressed my aunty, 'Don't let him back, or you go too. Jy lat hom nie weer hier innie. As jy hom trug vat soek jy anner plek.'

My aunty sobbed, the family stared at the scene.

My pa raised his voice one more time. 'Ko' jy net weer hier, ek maak jou vrek.'

The threat of imminent death must have seemed real. Chinky packed up and left. I never saw him again.

I remember relishing my dad's masculinity. It felt warm in his glow. My daddy had defeated the evil monster. The same way that my chastity honoured him, his masculinity elevated me in the early 2000 Coloured family dynamic. My daddy was the 'ou'.

I relayed this story many times, to my mom when we got home and to random people over the years.

I laughed at how pathetic and desperate for piel Brenda was and had always been. My father would never have to save me; I was refined – educated.

157

Okay, let's get back to living in my separate entrance, without my son, with charismatic, chronically unemployed Lyle.

Dating an abuser and living with one is very different. Behind the safety of walls and doors, they start to remove their mask more frequently. And by safety, I mean for them. They have the luxury of letting down the facade. Abuse, at least when it came to Lyle, was the need for control over everything, over me, his victim. His property. And a willingness to do anything, even lewd things to ensure that he remained in control, powerful.

From the moment we moved in in Lakeside, our relationship started to change. It declined for me, but I think for him it became better. I suddenly went from being his girlfriend, to something else; I don't have the proper word for it. I had even less freedom than when I lived with my parents. He was obsessed with us following the biblical parameters of a male/female relationship. Everything besides the main rule that we weren't to be sexual until marriage. I cleaned, I made all the food. He conveniently accepted that I made all the money – but I guess he had his own version of the Bible.

'We are Catholics, Shana,' he argued with me when I was honest about wanting to live on my own before we move in together. It was two nights into living in Westlake and I was on his blow-up mattress. I couldn't afford a bed, but I was fine with sleeping on the couch that came with the place.

'What does that have to do with anything?' I asked, confused.

'A Catholic woman can't live alone. She'll get up to mischief.' The way he wagged his finger, mimicking his grandfather, is stuck in my head. He kept his head high as if he had said something profound. He was proud of himself.

'But we aren't married. And you don't have a job to split bills.' I was hoping he would see the logic.

'Oh. That's why. Now you don't want to open your legs because I am not working at the moment. I thought we were a team. You just said that kak because you wanted me to leave Nadine.'

'What does sex have to do with anything?'

'It's true, man. You women just want material things.'

'I buy my own things.'

'Your daddy buy all your kak. You ma now have your first job. Where's your laaitie, man?' He was snarling at me, using my insecurities like knives. Everything I said was disqualified by something unrelated.

'What do you mean I wanted you to leave Nadine? You said you weren't seeing each other?' My nerves tingled.

'Jy, you know what I mean, man. You wanted me to leave that friendship because you were jealous.'

'That doesn't make sense.' I raised my voice.

'Hos, you don't shout at me.'

'But you lying to me!' I entered the boundaries of hysterical. He didn't know what I knew, but the fact that he was so blatantly lying in my face was fucking infuriating.

'Jy, don't start this kak again!' He exhaled, exasperated by my nagging.

Whenever I would bring up anything that bothered me, he was always visibly annoyed. Looking back, I can tell that he used annoyance to deter me from asking him anything about his transgressions. If I approached any subject he didn't feel like addressing, he took the argument to a 10 as a defense tactic – eventually I was too exhausted to broach anything in fear that I step on a conversational landmine and fuck up my own day.

'I was just asking you to explain what you meant.' I took my tone down by several notches.

'You fokken obsessed about this kin. Do you want me to naai

159

her?' He wasn't backing down. He had switched the conversational dynamic. I was now under scrutiny. The old bait and switch, an abuser classic.

'Now if you want me to go, then your poes. I'll phone my pa now to fetch me.'

He looked at me. I didn't say anything. I was so conflicted. I wanted him to go, but I didn't want to break up. I didn't object fast enough, apparently.

'And I will take all my kak I brought with me.'

He stood up and unplugged the bed I was lying on. It started to deflate instantly. I struggled to get up. I twisted and turned, looking for a spot that could bear my weight so that I could lift myself.

'Ja, get off there, jou naai. You gonna tear the whole thing. Then you gonna buy me a new one.'

He didn't offer a hand. I eventually found my feet and walked to the lounge. He followed me. The air was thinning out. He was volatile. I could feel the fragility of the situation, of his mood. His eyes were large, manic. The frustrated part of me wanted to argue and get my point across. But my fear kept me logical. He had hit me once before, but he had been drunk. I knew it wasn't part of his personality.

'And this plates is from my mommy's house.' He started to unpack the cupboard. He took the cutlery, crockery and a pan he had jacked from his home. 'Your mense gave you fokkol. They don't care what happens to you here. Don't forget that.'

He took out a tog bag from the cupboard and packed. He liked to tell me how my family didn't care about me. He constantly reminded me of the things I had confided in him when we were besties. It was strange how he remembered those parts, but not how he used to love me and compliment me. Or how we used to be besties.

'This is our two-plate.' He unplugged it.

I just sat there. Everything was moving so fast. We hadn't been drinking this time, but he was escalating the argument into a scene. 'Please talk softer, the landlord's house is right outside.' I looked through the front window.

'That man's poes, man. I have rights, I paid to be here.'

He didn't. I did. But saying that was suicide.

'. . . And I'm gonna phone your taani and tell her all the kak you wanna catch on. That's mos why you left your laaitie at home. You a kak mother.'

'How can you say that?' I started to cry. I sat on the couch and cried, silently, into the palms of my hand. My eyes were so full of tears I couldn't see. My face, neck and collar were soaked.

I watched Lyle stomp around the space, rolling like a street gangster as he made his way through the cupboards. He walked as if he were on a catwalk, throwing his shoulders and wiping his nose with his thumb. Just pure bravado packing a bag.

'It's mos true.' The cupboards slammed between words. 'You wanted to jintoe. You didn't leave them for me, your future husband. You then don't want me here. You left to party.'

'I didn't say I don't want you here. I can't live with a man. My parents won't approve,' I tried to package it kindly.

'Jy, your parents gran me, man. They know you not a virgin.' He took his phone. His bag was packed now and he sat on the couch opposite.

I watched him, nervous.

'I am gonna phone my pa now. But yoh, they said bye to me yesterday, now I must go back home. That is kak embarrassing.' He looked down at his hands, his eyes down. 'I am gonna be in the eyes, wow Shana, are you really going to do this to me?'

I didn't want to answer him. I didn't want him there, but now

161

I wasn't sure why. Why wouldn't I want my boyfriend there? Was I being immoral and selfish? Perhaps sending him home was cruel. If he left, would he go back to Nadine? I knew he would find someone quickly and I would be jealous and alone. What if this was my chance to get married? Maybe living together would make us close again. He had never lived with a woman before, so this might be what changes him. I could take full credit for taming this beast.

He started crying. A man, crying. This was a breakthrough. I watched him sob. I couldn't believe it.

'Do you want me to leave because of the other night?'

He looked at me, eyes red and face wet. I was thrilled that he had brought it up. It obviously meant that it was bothering him.

'Yes, you made me scared,' I got up and went to sit down next to him. I relished this rare, tender moment. It was my time to shine as a maternal figure. A caregiver. A woman. I could be his peace.

'I'm really not like that, Shana. I was dik gesuip, out of it and you hit me first. You must also take blame. We had a fight. All couples do that.'

He moved away from me on the couch. 'Come on now, you know me. You then my bra, before all of this.'

I smiled, now fully immersed in the romanticism. The reality of how he had treated me since that night faded. I agreed, I was a difficult person. My mom and sister had always said so. Many of my teachers had shared the same sentiments. Perhaps it would be mature of me to acknowledge it. Personal growth.

I hugged him. 'You can stay. I'm sorry for upsetting you.'

'Ja,' he nodded.

He picked up his bag and stood up. 'Na, I'm gonna go.'

'No, please stay. I want to work on us.'

162

He looked at me, deadpan. As suddenly as the tears had flowed down his face, they had stopped.

'Don't ask me to leave again. Because I will.' His shoulders were square and held high again. His chest peacocking.

'I won't.' I didn't realise that I was basically kneeling off the side of the couch.

He turned and went to unpack.

I felt relieved that I had dodged having to relive the last few months when he left the first time. I'd won, for now.

In the next few weeks, I fell very quickly into a pseudo-married lifestyle. Well, sort of. We slept in the same bed. We lived as man and wife. But I never felt as if we had a home. It always felt like an uncanny valley version of happily ever after. Every day after work, I would come home to him playing video games and drinking beers on the couch.

'You late,' he would say if I came home five minutes off the schedule he had worked out.

I was always nervous that anything I said or did would throw the equilibrium of the relationship. I lived in constant anxiety about spoiling everything, much as I had lived at home, but this space was more fragile. In my mother's house, if I did something bad, she could reprimand me, but she would still be my mother. A man could leave at any time. And then one day, I worked overtime and needed a lift home from a colleague. She and her boyfriend wanted to come inside and I called Lyle to let him know. Can you imagine, getting permission in my own home. He didn't answer. When we stopped outside, I was inexplicably nervous – nervous to allow guests into my own fucking place. I told them I just wanted to go inside first and check that everything was okay. So awkward – I don't think they understood what that meant. They were normal people who were too polite to ask.

I unlocked the gate and made my way to the front door, more slowly than usual. I was planning what I would say to justify having people over.

When I opened the door, Lyle was sitting in the lounge, looking at me. The TV was off. He must have been sitting there, just staring at the door, waiting.

'Where were you, jou naai?' he greeted.

'What do you mean?' I shivered.

'You end work at 5pm, it's almost 7 o' clock. Are you taking me for a poes?'

'I messaged you.'

'Jy, any naai can send messages, man. Didn't you see I didn't answer you?'

'But I had to work late. Why are you going on like this?'

'You a jintoe, that's why. Since the night I met you, remember? You permy lie.'

'Lyle, my colleague wants to come in. Please calm down. We can discuss it later.'

'Your colleague? Since when are you friends with colleagues? A bra?' He stood up. His eyebrow was raised and his fist was clenched.

I stood back. 'No a white kin.' That seemed like the least threatening way to describe her.

'Say they must maarts, go.'

'What do you mean?'

I barely got the words out before she came to the door.

'Shana?' She peeked in.

I turned with a smile. 'Hey,' was all I could manage. My mind went blank.

'Hi there,' she said to Lyle. He didn't change his expression. He mean mugged her and shoved past her to go look who was in her car.

164

I couldn't move, I didn't know what was going to happen.

She was rightfully puzzled by the Neanderthal who couldn't use his words. 'Is everything okay?'

'Yes, he just feels sick.'

'Did he take something?'

'Yes,' I grabbed the lifeline. 'He is having a bad reaction to his meds.'

'Ag shame, no man. We can hang out some other time then. Totally understand . . . ' She rambled something about her boy-friend but I was already at the gate.

Lyle was standing at the front wall, staring at the guy.

She got into the car and smiled. They drove off.

'Why did you do that to me? I work with those people.'

'Hou jou bek and go inside.'

'What? I'm not fucking going inside. Why are you being like a psycho?'

He seemed to like that I had used that word. Psycho. His eyes went big and he turned his head to the side. I felt embarrassed for him. It was so childish. It was the first time I recognised that I was dating below my level of evolution, although I didn't have words for it yet. I had seen this behaviour with most Coloured boys. An afshoweragge, 'I'm a mal naai I promise' persona, to cover up how damaged but still uninteresting they are. I didn't know that it could spill over into Coloured manhood though.

I rolled my eyes. 'What are you doing?' I walked past him, through the yard, into my place. I sat down and switched on the TV. I heard a loud bang outside. He had pulled off a section of the wooden gate and the sound was the thick wood popping as it snapped in two. He walked towards the house, holding the baton.

'Woah, wah, wat gat hier aan?' An older man came out of the

main house, bothered by the noise. 'Wat maak jy met my broer se huis?'

Lyle stood up close to this uncle and I watched through the window.

'This piece came off the gate . . . ' He suddenly wasn't a sideways psycho anymore. He was coherent and non-aggressive.

'Julle skree heel aand hier agter.'

I felt sick.

'Naai, that wasn't us, uncle. We stil mense, quiet, don't mix, you see?' He looked around, his eyebrow raised. That mental audience must have been giving him a standing ovation. I watched, but didn't hear anything more. It seemed de-escalated and I was happy that the incident had snapped him out of his tantrum.

I took my Blackberry out to phone Sidney. I missed him. I searched for my mom's contact. She had called me earlier that week, to check on me I think, under the guise of telling me my son was asking for me. She had kept me on the phone for longer than usual. I had promised to call Sidney before the weekend.

The punch hit the back of my head. I heard it as I felt it. His fist landed on the back, but something atop my head sounded as if it snapped open. The inside of my forehead pounded as I fell forward. My eyes were open, but everything was spinning. I couldn't tense my lips to close them. My saliva had never felt so runny.

I reached for my phone, but he picked it up and hurled it at the wall.

It was the first time I had ever seen the inside layers of a phone. The metal sheets clanked as the shattered phone fell against the broken glass on the tiled floor.

I found my bearings and looked at Lyle. He was still moving from left to right. The whole room was.

166

'Help!' I shouted. I didn't shout loud enough for anyone to hear. I didn't want to get him into trouble, I just wanted him to stop.

He leaped forward and grabbed my face. His hand wrapped around my lips and chin and his fingertips dug into my cheeks. He crushed my jaw. I couldn't breathe.

I fought back, but gently. I didn't want to hurt him. It is hard to explain. A person with empathy doesn't just use full force, even in self-defense. There is still the fear of hurting the abuser, a human being. Compassion can kill you.

He used his free hand to grip my hair. He pulled it hard. I felt a gap between my skull and my scalp stretch open. Strands of hair started to tear out of my scalp. Still holding me up by my hair, he released my jaw. I gulped air.

I didn't shout, though. I just needed to get through whatever this tantrum was so that we could go back to normal. He wasn't a violent person.

He carried me this way till we reached the wall. He shoved my face towards the rough red brick.

I kept my neck stiff.

He could have easily overpowered me, but he didn't. I noticed that he wasn't using his full strength. And I resisted, but mildly. A strange moment of limbo in which he staved off his animal instincts and I was tricked into believing I was safe.

I fell to the floor, free. I was sobbing, holding my head to soothe the pain. Every part of my face and head burned.

He walked past me to the bedroom and lay down. He fell asleep.

I sat there on the floor for hours. Just thinking. And not thinking. And thinking.

I pieced my phone back together. The screen didn't work well, it jumped between the cracks but I was able to call my son. He couldn't speak fluently yet, but hearing him say 'I love you, Mama' was enough to break my heart.

I sat in the dark, unable to get myself to switch the light on. I heard a rustling. The toilet flushed and Lyle came back. My heart raced, but I sat still. He switched on the light and stared at me on the floor.

'Hey baby. Yoh, how long did I sleep? When did you get back from work?'

The weeks that followed were uneventful. Lyle had no recollection of the commotion. He told me that he had taken cough mixture that morning and the rest was a blur. I was fascinated that I had used that as an excuse for his behaviour to my friend. I kept wondering whether he had mentioned it to me over the phone that day or whether I had lied loudly enough for him to hear. On the weekend I went to see my son for a few hours. It was the only place I was allowed to go without him. After a month, my parents gave me back my car to make it easier to get to work.

During the week, Lyle would fight with me each morning, or force me to have sex before leaving, even after I was showered and dressed. He would say that I had a car now, so I could get back into bed, I didn't need to be early. At first, I would argue that I wanted to get a head start on the day's work, or beat traffic, but on the days I didn't sleep with him he would be moody and ignore my texts, or not speak to me when I got home. So, I would have sex each morning and wait five minutes, in his arms, until he fell asleep. I would wash and leave, until he told me he didn't want me to shower after the sex. It was his insurance policy that my vagina was soiled – by him. I would go to work with a smelly crotch. I always went in late. On most days I was self-conscious.

He would hide my car keys on the days he was particularly horny.

168

I was fired pretty quickly. But I found another job soon, although it paid less.

'Please try to find a job, I can't afford everything anymore,' I asked him one day. It had been a calm day, so I took a chance on bringing up the issue. I did my best to keep my voice low and non-confrontational. He was sensitive about not bringing in cash and didn't like when I spoke of money.

'I sent my CV the whole week, no one is replying to me, Shana.' He was in the bathroom shaving. I was sorting my cupboard for the week. It was a Sunday night and my new job started the next day.

'I know, but maybe try different types of jobs?' I moved the stacks of folded items to the drawer. We were being cordial. We had been mostly okay for the while. He was nice to me for the most part. I felt confident we could have a normal conversation about the future. He walked out from the bathroom, in a towel.

'Can I go in? I must still do my hair.' I continued what I was doing. I placed my sprays, eyeliner and lipstick on the dressing table. I set out my brushes and clips to blow my hair and adjusted the mirror. I bent over to plug in the hair dryer. Between my legs, I saw his towel drop to the floor. He grabbed my hips and pretended to thrust into me. I laughed. It was cute and playful.

I stood up to grab my stuff to go shower. He didn't let go of my hips. He thrust again. I laughed again, although I wasn't as tickled the second time.

He hit me with his pelvis, over and over. I looked in the mirror. He wasn't smiling. He pounded against me, his tongue hanging loosely out his mouth. I didn't like that. I pulled away.

'Where you going?' He was breathing heavily. This was the first time I felt violated. He looked like an animal on heat.

'I want to wash me. I need to make myself right for work.' I

169

squeezed past him. I didn't make eye contact. I got to the bathroom. I put my towel and products on the toilet and turned on
the shower. He walked in.

'No ways,' he said and pulled me out the bathroom with one
hand. With the other, he closed the taps.

'What the fuck?' I stood naked in the passage.

'You can mos never leave me hanging like that, ek sê.' He came
towards me and placed a hand on my cheek. He was being both
authoritative and gentle. I flinched even before his hand touched
my face.

'Are you bang for me now – you scared?' He looked hurt, offended. 'Yoh, you take me by the gevriet.' He didn't move out of
my personal space, though.

'No. No, I'm not. I'm just getting ready.' I was stuttering and
shivering.

'Nah, I can see you don't even want me to touch you anymore.'
He let me go. I moved back towards the bathroom but he stopped
me with the inside of his forearm.

'Stry tog?' His face was a millimetre away from mine as he
asked me if I wanted a fight.

'No, I just want to bath.' I stood dead still. I was trying to control my muscles and not shake.

'Now why do you want to fight me, man. Keeping you sterk.
Relax, let your body wobble,' he laughed. He was teasing me, but
it felt violent.

'Lyle, I just want to get done for tomorrow, please.'

'For what? Why do you need to do your hair for work?'

'I need to look professional. It's my first day.'

'Kak praat. Who did you see by the interview? Weer reg brasse
daar.'

Standing there, naked, freezing, I wanted to sob in frustration. I looked around with my eyes – I couldn't move my head because of the way he was blocking me.

'Jy, stop looking around when I'm talking to you, man.' He headbutted me between the eyes. The teeth in my top jaw zinged. They felt loose. I bit down to stop the sensation. Pain was shooting in bursts from my forehead through to the back of my head.

'Focus jy, man.' He didn't let go.

'Now come, we're talking. Why are you scared of me?'

He used that daddy tone again. Whenever this part of him took over, he was an authority. He wore his power powerfully, proudly. I didn't know how to make him listen. I stood there, trying desperately to get through the pain and open my eyes.

'Okay, you want something to be scared of, then here we go.'

He grabbed me by the arm with one hand, but it was enough of a grip on the right place for him to manoeuvre my body with ease. He led me to the bed. And pulled me down so that I would sit.

I sat there, exhausted, a little bored by having to deal with his tantrums and terrified. The breaks between his trips were getting shorter. I knew he was trying to control his temper most of the time. But this time was so inconvenient. He went out of the room and I heard the clanking of the opening and closing cutlery drawer. My stomach turned. The contents of my bowels felt like hot liquid and they threatened to come out fast and runny. I remember thinking about jumping through the window and calling for help, but I was naked and didn't want the landlord to think I was stupid and childish.

He came back in carrying my kitchen scissors. They looked ominous in his hands. He gave a few preliminary snips. The sound was sharp and squeaky. They sounded like they would deliver a clean, fast cut.

'You wanna look lekker tomorrow you say?'

He walked to my drawer. He took the clothes that I had just packed and grabbed a handful of them, destroying my hard work. He placed the pile on the dresser. 'Come we see where you go with no clothes.'

He snipped through the sleeves. I just sat and watched. He cut through each one, then went down to the floor and sat by my shoes. He cut the straps of every sandal.

'Please stop,' I cried. I tried to remain calm. I knew by now that crying and being hysterical did not invoke empathy in him, it fuelled him. The more devastated I was, the more powerful he felt. It made him hurt me harder. Though, the less emotion I showed, the harder he tried to be cruel. I had no control over any of it. No matter what I did, I was in danger. At this point I was starting to plan how I would leave him, but I was also constantly fighting thoughts about why I should stay. In my mind, all my aunties had this type of relationship in the beginning. I knew men were supposed to be tamed, but I was also in two minds about whether this level of struggle was normal. I know my uncles were all abusive, but as they got older and got used to the idea of being married and becoming fathers, they usually started to surrender. We just needed to cross the middle line. I know my mom was abusive when I was younger, but she too calmed down over the years. I just needed to wait. Giving up on this relationship, after making such big moves to save it would be a failure: embarrassing. Besides, he wasn't going to kill me. He didn't always hit me either. He didn't even remember the first two times. It was that fucking medication and alcohol.

'Stop? Make me stop, man. I'm a mal naai.' He kept snipping things.

'I am not challenging you, I'm begging you. I need clothes for work. We need the money.'

'Money, money,' he mocked me. 'You treat me like a poes because I don't have money.'

'No I don't,' I wanted to get up but he turned to me, pointing the closed scissors at my face.

'It is, sien jy. But you jas.' He came closer. 'I am still the man here.'

'I never said you weren't, Lyle.'

His lips curled. 'You don't have to say it, I know how females think. Money, skit, lekker joint. You all just fucking gold diggers.'

Lyle straddled my lap and pushed my shoulders back. I landed on my back on the bed. He put the blade of the scissor on my face. He grimaced and showed his teeth, then stopped. Then again, then stopped. He looked as if he was having an argument in his head.

'I'm gonna naai you now,' he said, in a calm voice.

'No, I don't want to please', I thought, but I didn't say. I just lay there. I couldn't move. I just wanted to play possum until it was over.

He laid his body flat against mine. Skin to skin, his chest scratched my nipples. The lights were on and the curtains were open.

Every part of his body was inexplicably warm, hot. He was resting on me. The scissors were still in his hand.

He thrust into me, harder than he ever had. My vagina was dry at first. His penis pulled the skin of my entrance. It burned as he went in and out, not waiting for me to get wet. I groaned in agony. The sides of my vagina burned like acid had been poured into me. After a minute or so, I felt the wetness come to save me. His pelvis hit my G-spot, but my vagina felt pleasure while the rest of my body tensed. I couldn't stop the orgasm, but I didn't want it.

'Lekker, ne.' His mouth hung open, jaw relaxed and he took his last, deep, deliberate strokes. He let his spit run into my face as he panted.

He remained on me after he came. 'Didn't that feel great?'

I said nothing.

'And don't come talk kak about rape, you were kak wet. You came paar times,' he spoke again.

I hadn't even considered that I was being raped. I didn't know your boyfriend or husband could rape you. I had chosen to live with a man, I should have known better. This is what big people did. Grown women stuff.

He went to sleep. I went to shower. But I didn't cry. From that night I no longer cried, or got scared. I felt very little, actually. I didn't want to feel anymore.

My phone notifications woke me up around 2am, Lyle was gone. He had taken my card and locked me in the room. I watched as he swiped for hundreds of rands at the random bars in Muizenberg. He spent the rest of that night drinking up my savings at Toad on the Road.

Eventually, the landlord asked us to leave the place. He had been complaining about noise and he and Lyle argued about what was and wasn't allowed on the property. We looked online for options. My mother had asked me to move back in with them. I didn't know, but my family had planned an intervention. I couldn't risk going back to my old life though. It was a different type of imprisonment. At least with Lyle I could drink and smoke. Naaing was a small price to pay to experience being 'young' again. I didn't want to be with my child either. I missed him dearly, but I wasn't a mother, I was trash. I pitied Sidney for the card he had been dealt. Everyone else had seen my uselessness. Soon, he would also see that I wasn't good. At anything.

It's hard to pinpoint what makes you an adult in a Coloured family. Beyond being outright incompetent and broken, I also still didn't see myself as an adult, even though I had a child. Not in my parents' house. I didn't actually have authority over my child. My mom decided everything for my baby. I needed her permission to take him anywhere. I couldn't make decisions about what he ate, or even what time he went to bed. I couldn't say no to him because I was still a laaitie. I was my child's equal because in my mother's eyes, I was still an unmarried child. This was perpetuated by other extended family members who felt that I had somehow wronged them personally for being unchaste. Some would even go as far as to reprimand me for 'putting their aunt and uncle in this position'. I have one irritating memory of my cousin asking me if she could give Sidney some Panado. I said yes, to which she replied, 'Oh, I asked your mommy rather and she said I mustn't give him.' And that ended the conversation, because my spine hadn't grown in yet.

I didn't want to go back to that.

While we searched for a new place, Lyle said he needed to speak to me about an idea for his new business plan. He had told me one day, excitedly, that he was ready to get back into making money. Strangely this came when I was close to leaving him for the first time. Now he said he wanted to help me with the bills and build a real future. He wanted to start a BMX customisation company but he just needed me to help him with capital. He couldn't take out a loan while he was unemployed, so I had to get him R25 000 and he would pay it back to me.

The morning that we moved out of the separate entrance, the money reflected in my account. My mother said that Lyle could come with me and live with them while we looked for our next place. I agreed, because it seemed like she was finally onboard

175

with me being a grown-up – and it was a temporary situation. It was certainly out of character, but I was desperate. They assumed that he and I would be married and I guess I liked the idea of my BF being allowed to sleep in my bed at my parents' home. It felt like they had accepted my grown-upness a bit. I only see now my mother wanted me nearby so she could save me from Lyle: I wish she had been straight with me, although at the time I would have rejected her assistance. I would have seen it as inter-ference instead of what it really was, motherly care. To save face I bought my own engagement ring. I gave it to Lyle and he pro-posed to me in a small sushi shop in Blue Route mall. He went down on both knees, though. I should have known right there that he was crazy.

Living with my parents went sour pretty quickly. Lyle didn't want Sidney in our room. Kinders slapie met groot mense nie. I never argued. He would throw tantrums in a whisper and threaten me with embarrassment to get his way. I think he en-joyed seeing how much he could coerse me into doing.

One evening, Lyle locked our bedroom door and told me to strip naked or he would make a scene and naai me in front of my daddy. I lay there, naked on my blankets, while he watched porn on a TV he made me buy and pleasured himself. I couldn't help sobbing. My parents heard and demanded I open the door, but he wouldn't let me get dressed. I chose to keep the door closed instead of asking for help.

The next day he kept me in the room and, when my parents left to take Sidney to crèche, he hit me to the floor. He packed his bag and said he was leaving. I begged him to stay.

But when my parents came back, my dad told him to leave. The neighbours had caught them on the way up to the apartment, to say that it sounded like someone was being beaten up in the room upstairs. I was angry that the neighbours had interfered. But Lyle left happily – he didn't even try to fight for us.

In the aftermath I had to endure being scolded for allowing him to abuse me: I was stupid for letting someone violate me and weak for being sad that the relationship was over.

I was sad for a long time and the longer I didn't see him, the less I thought of the abuse, which at the time I hadn't seen as abuse, only as his personality. I got used to my new life and not seeing him, though. He ignored my phone calls and seemed to have moved on.

It hurt, but I threw myself into other things. Until he called again one day to say he missed me.

My mother and father wouldn't hear any of it. He wanted me back, but I had made the mistake of letting other people in on our fights – now because of that mistake we couldn't be together anymore!

So, I saw him secretly. I would sneak off from work to go see him, or I would lie and say that I was working on my off days and drive to him. He wanted to have so much sex whenever we got together. More than usual. I was so flattered by how much he seemed to have missed my body.

Pretty quickly, I fell pregnant. And everything fell to shit again.

I decided immediately that I would have an abortion.

Lyle didn't like the idea that I wanted to abort his flesh and blood. He had no job and we weren't even allowed to see each other because of me . . . but he said that the baby was from God, a reason why people couldn't keep us apart anymore. I regretted telling him about my decision. He asked me how I could keep an unwanted child like Sidney, whose dad didn't care, but I had the heart to kill his child. I didn't know what answer to give to that question, to him or to myself.

177

Now I sat on the stoep of his grandpa's house and watched as he took out his phone to tell my parents.

'No, please don't do that,' I jumped up to grab his phone.

He pushed me on my chest. He put his phone in his pocket.

I got up and walked to my car.

He ran up behind me. 'Where you going?'

'Home,' I said. I opened the car door.

'You don't want my baby?' He was gentle again.

I looked in his eyes. They were so calm and puppy-dog soft. Maybe he was ready to hear my side.

'No. I can't afford . . .'

Lyle spat a massive ball of mucous into my face. It hit me hard enough to make me jump back. It landed on my nose, in my eyes and on my lips.

'Just you hurt my laaitie, you see me hurt yours.'

I didn't even wipe my face. I climbed in the car and locked the door. I didn't drive away, though. He was still talking.

'I love you, Shana. Don't dala this kak. Abortion is against our religion.'

I started the car and maneuvered it around him slowly. He didn't move.

I wiped the spit off my face at the first robot. I cried all the way to Kenilworth. I felt so confused about my life, but I knew I didn't want to go back to him. I wasn't going to have another baby with another deadbeat. I was going to take charge of my future, no matter what.

When I got home, my parents knew I was pregnant. I had the abortion anyway and said that I had miscarried. I was done with Lyle. I deleted him, blocked him.

I found a new job and after four months of being strong I opened my email to a love letter he had written me. He was a changed man. He saw the error of his ways and wanted to see me one last time to apologize in person and give our separation closure.

So, I met him, wrapped in all my newfound success and over him completely.

One month later, I was pregnant with Syria-Rose, on purpose.

# Chapter 11

# Round 2. Fight.

While I was pregnant with Syria-Rose I came close to suicide. I toyed with the idea of suffocating Sidney and then poisoning myself. The problem was that it wasn't the 1800s and poison wasn't exactly readily available. The risk for injury that came with drinking something as plebeian as bleach was too high.

At the beginning of this pregnancy my family moved back to our Pelican Heights home. I was now a 24-year-old single mom, pregnant again and back at my parents' home. I lived in the spare room, amidst boxes and extra cupboards and things. On a single bed, with my son, awaiting the arrival of my daughter.

I had left Lyle again when I was just a month along. Every night since, I sat in the dark, just thinking. I would put Sidney to sleep and open my curtain to look onto the road. There was a streetlamp right across from my window and I just sat and stared at the spot of tar it illuminated. Hours of staring. Thinking. Replaying my life in my head. Looking at Sidney. Staring at him. He slept next to me so peacefully. He trusted me completely, even as I consciously fucked up his life. Our life. In my nightly evaluations of what my life had become, I couldn't understand how I was so smart, but kept making the worst decisions. I didn't understand why every avenue for success I engaged in failed miserably. And I couldn't understand how everything I built, every part of myself that I improved, I was willing to give away the second someone was romantically interested in me. Like two people lived inside my consciousness. One who fucked up every opportunity I was given, just to avoid loneliness, and one who watched me sabotage everything, just appalled at the aftermath.

In the evenings, I would pray to Jesus that the baby in my womb would die, or that Sidney would die – in an incident that wasn't my fault. I wanted to be absolved of my sins. The only way that could happen was if I started on a clean slate and the world pitied me. If something happened to my kids, I would forever be a martyr – a woman who had come upon horrendous times. A survivor. But now I was nothing more than a hoe with babies.

I made promises to God that if I could start over and redo my life, I would never touch a man again. I even had waking nightmares of getting my second chance and then falling for Lyle again. When I imagined these scenarios, I would scream out loud, as if to shake off the dread, the imagined regret. I had enough real regret, way too much to be stressing over imaginary regret too. My body didn't have the space for it.

For the first two weeks of my pregnancy with Syria-Rose, Lyle was great. It felt as if my friend was back. We made a few plans; the normal fluff talk that couples do when they feel extra in love. The positive pregnancy test felt different this time. I had wanted to fall pregnant, I admit, out of guilt for having the last abortion. I didn't quite know how I was going to play it to my family, but I knew I couldn't stand the flashbacks of the doctor sucking up the pregnancy with that pipe. I honestly thought having a baby would absolve me somehow – I can see now that I wasn't as mentally healthy as I thought I was. I was still suffering. In part a sort of post-abortion depression that I hadn't expected.

Regardless, we spoke about getting a place of our own again, as soon as he got a permanent job. I was so excited – I was almost proud of what a smart move this was, to have a baby.

Very soon, he began to hit me again. Now, he would only aim for the face. It was more slaps when I was cheeky than full-on punches, but they stung more for some reason. He slapped me in the same way one would slap a rude child across the lips. He did it with the back of his hand, nonchalantly. He didn't give it much thought.

Suddenly, one day, something inside of me stopped wanting him. I felt numb towards him. It was like an epiphany, as if the pregnancy hormones cleared my mind. But two weeks too late. I messaged him that I was done with the relationship. I wished him well and said that I didn't want to see him anymore.

Again, a sense of determination came over me. I had started a new job and threw myself into work. When I got home, I would spend time with Sidney, watch movies, be pregnant. My moves were intentional and even though I knew the world was disgusted by me, I was determined that this would be my turning point. And it was, for a bit.

Lyle wasn't as easily swayed. He started the love bombing phase all over again. The fact that I had his growing child in my stomach seemed to give him an ownership over me and he was outraged that I no longer wanted him. In his misogynistic mind, he had marked me.

It was flattering and off-putting at the same time. He was trying so hard, so late. I would wake up to Lyle standing outside of my window, blasting 'I'm gonna marry her anyway' through his pa's car speakers. Don't get me wrong, he was by no means offering me romance and a proper future. Rather, his disdain for me had turned into some sort of toxic obsession. He messaged me night and day and called me between the messages. If I didn't answer, my phone would fill up with missed calls and emails that ran for pages, days. How Cell C managed to deliver anyone else's telecommunication is a goddamn mystery.

And most days, it was as if I was being texted by two different men. One who loved me obsessively and one who was angry with me for him loving me obsessively.

In the morning I would wake up to 'morning baby. I know I mustn't call you baby, but you carrying my baby – LOL'. In the afternoon it would be, 'Jy jou naai answer my texts you know how I am. I soema get worried sien jy, don't be a poes. Just answer once then I know you and my laaitie is safe. That's all you have to do. Don't make this difficult.'

By the time I was six months pregnant, the harassment was still going on, but he had gotten himself a new girlfriend. This was a punishment for me leaving him (his sentiments, not mine). The texts were all about her and how he was over me and my bullshit. I must admit, I was jealous that while I carried his baby, he had set his sights on someone else. Again.

He constantly berated me for 'seeing his worth too late, only after another woman had appreciated him'. A real woman who took care of herself and didn't have laaities by everyone, he would say. She would dictate when he could see me, or whether or not he would spend money on anything I needed to prepare for the baby. Now that I think about it, he may have just said that to make my experience as bad as possible. She probably didn't even know I existed.

To add the CheryQQ3 on top, her name was Nadine too.

The trauma of doing the nine months alone again left me a wreck. So, by the seven-month mark, I allowed him to see me. I even agreed that he could come with me to an ultrasound and

183

I will admit the idea that the father of my baby would be by my side was exciting. Alas, it was again the uncanny valley version that just wasn't quite right.

At the gynaecologist's, I looked around at the other pregnant women. Their husbands sat next to them holding their hands, or rubbing their backs. Some of the women were dressed in the gorgeous maternity wear I had seen in catalogues. Others had brought their other kids along. I particularly envied a family who sat opposite us: she was very pregnant and he was entertaining their three-year-old, leaving her to sit back and relax. I had never relaxed, not as a mom. Not in my whole life. I teared up, wiping my eyes as soon as the tears formed.

Lyle sat next to me, on his phone. We hadn't really spoken since I had picked him up. Before he got into the car he had leaned in to kiss me and stuck his tongue in my mouth. When I pulled away, he just laughed and said, 'Wat gat jy soe aan, jy's dan kla pregnant', as he reclined the seat and lay down. He didn't say anything else to me, just chatted and laughed at the screen. All the way. When I sat down next to him after I paid the bill upfront at the secretary's counter he didn't even look at me. It bothered me. Even though he wasn't my boyfriend, I expected some sort of compassion, or at least maternity waiting room etiquette.

'Can you please stop chatting while we are here?' I whispered in my meekest tone.

He tilted his phone screen away from me. 'Why? Must we go in?' He pressed 'send'.

'Who are you be speaking to that is more important than this?'

'That's none of your business,' he laughed. He wasn't whispering, so everyone was looking at us.

'It's fine. We need to talk about the loan. I need you to help me start paying it back before Syria comes.' I wanted to speak about something else.

'Jas!' he laughed louder than he had sworn. 'You helped me eat that money out.'

'Please lower your voice.'

He leaned back and pointed at my face, ironically quieter now.

'Jy, your poes, man. And this mense's poes,' he whispered. 'Must I wys you I shout? Don't think cos you are pregnant you have control. I'll pay you back my half, or what I can, when I can, niks else.'

I stood up to go outside. I exited the door and stood in the passageway. He came out behind me, still on his phone.

'Hey baby, I am just checking if you awake . . .'

He had called Nadine. I went back inside, smiling at everyone to compensate for the commotion. I just sat there, sad smiling with the tears streaming down my neck.

When it was our turn we went inside and went through the motions of the ultrasound. When he saw Syria on the screen I saw a glimpse of his humanity again. A shadow of the Lyle I had met passed over his face. He placed his hand on my leg gently and stared, enamoured, at the screen.

'Yoh, that's really my laaitie.' The doctor smiled and went out the room for a minute to give us some time to just bask in the beauty of nature.

'Tell me now, Shana, is this another bra's child? Tell me now?'

That would forever be my first experience of pregnancy with the father by my side. Right there I vowed that I would never have a baby again.

At the end of the appointment, I told the gynaecologist to add a tubal ligation to my C-section. After answering a few questions about whether my future husband would mind my being barren, he agreed.

Then, like a move into the Twilight zone, something strange happened.

185

For that last month of my pregnancy, Lyle was a gentleman. He started taking on odd jobs and began bringing me treats. I couldn't understand it and deep down I didn't trust it. I saw the pattern of happy and rude, kind and evil that he kept repeating. But again, I somehow fell into it. This time it was the loneliness though, 100 per cent. It felt so lekker to have a man, the father of my child, bring me things to eat. He would ask me what I craved and then bring it right and left. I really enjoyed my mother seeing me being treated 'well' while pregnant. It validated the pregnancy, sort of.

When I was pregnant with Sidney, she had said, 'Haai, jy hettie eers nou 'n man wat vir jou iets lekker kan koepie', and that had stuck with me. Yes, I knew bitterly that I didn't have a man to look after me and buy me nice things. I carried that embarrassment, reminding myself that other people noticed what I lacked. And worse, they could see what I so bitterly desired.

Lyle visited me weekly. In a compromise, my parents had said he wasn't allowed in the house, but he could see me in the garage. So, on Saturdays, he would come from his girlfriend's house and we would have sex in the garage. Pregnancy made me horny and he was always willing to oblige. I'd never had pregnancy sex in my first pregnancy, so I had looked forward to it. Although like most things it wasn't as I had imagined. Bending over the car in the garage while someone else's boyfriend fucked me raw wasn't the exact fantasy, but I was so sad and alone that I was willing to take any sort of touch I could get.

Then it was time to give birth.

The morning of Syria's C-section, Lyle was supposed to get a car to take me to the hospital. We were to be there at 8am. At 6am, he told me that he hadn't been able to secure a vehicle.

My mom dropped us both at the entrance to the hospital. I carried my own bag into the foyer.

The nurses prepped me for the C-Section – and for my sterili-sation. Before my operation, in the waiting area, Lyle stood with me. He was holding my hand. It had been years since he held my hand. I lay there quietly, basking in the moment. I was back here, four years later. About to have another child. I couldn't believe it. This time I wasn't with my mom, though. My man was next to me. I felt lekker, proud. But anxious.

The doctor approached me. A different doctor than my gy-naecologist; they were a team of obstetricians who would deliver babies depending on a shift schedule or something. I don't have the semantics, but in Coloured hospitals, even if you have an appointment and medical aid, you sit all day because they book as many people as they can. It's a waiting game, under the guise of private care.

'Hello, are you Ms Genever?'

'I am.'

He looked at me and then looked at his clipboard. 'You're very young.' He looked at me again. 'Are you sure you want to be sterilised? I am going to give you a few minutes to make sure,' he said and walked away.

I looked at Lyle. 'Should I be sterilised?'

'Yes,' he said instantly.

I remember thinking. 'Wow he didn't hesitate'.

He whispered in an even lower voice, laughing, 'Then we can mos . . .'

I knew the doctor could hear him. I was embarrassed, but laughed to make as if our relationship was this way, instead of showing him that I was allowing this lesser being to disrespect me.

I was about to call the doctor, when a woman I had never seen before approached me.

187

'My girl. Don't mean to pry.' She looked at me as I assumed a mother looked at a child she loved. 'I heard now that you want to sterilise you, but you are so young,' she said and put a hand on my shoulder. Her presence pushed Lyle out of the way as if she didn't even see him. 'Are you married?'

'No,' I kept her gaze. We were looking in each other's eyes.

'No, you still have a long life ahead. What if you meet some-one? What if you want another baby in future?' She stared at me. She was serious. Couldn't she see I was worthless and that none of that fairytale shit was going to happen to me?

'I have a son,' I said.

'So? Children are a blessing. You must still meet the love of your life.'

I couldn't stop the tears. Sadness spilled from my body.

'Can I pray for you?'

'Yes.'

I lay there and let this stranger lay her hands on me. It was the most comfort I had felt in my whole life, bar none. A woman, just pouring feminine love and energy into me, purposefully. For no reason but to bless me. Empower me. She squeezed me when she was done and walked away. The doctor returned.

'Sterilisation?' His maleness fucked up the vibe.

'No.'

Lyle looked at me, annoyed.

'I don't want more laaities,' he said.

I didn't either. But I didn't know at the time that I just didn't want more with him.

I have no memory of the C-section besides the doctors looking at him as Syria came out of me.

'Say thank you to your wife,' they said.

He looked at them with that snarl I had come to know, but he then turned his eyes to Syria and his face softened. He turned to me last and kissed me on the forehead.

'Thanks,' he said and walked out.

The anesthetic pulled out by the time I was wheeled from the waiting area to my room. In the waiting area he had sat next to me, chatting on his phone. He took pictures of Syria and shared them, writing about how proud he was of her and what a great job I had done. I lay there, under the white blankets, exhausted. Alone. My family didn't come to see me.

When we got to the room, I was in agony. I groaned uncontrollably because it helped relieve the pressure. The nurse brought Syria to me. I tried to lift myself up, using the side bars and slipped. My stomach muscles were finished, on account of being hacked into with a surgeon's blade.

'Help me,' I whispered. My abdomen was too sore for me to make more than a strong, bassy whisper. Lyle looked up from his phone and stood up. He grabbed my elbow and lifted me with one hand. His strength was impressive, dare I say attractive when he wasn't using it to smash me to the ground. And sometimes also when he was using it to smash me to the ground.

'Thank you.' I made myself comfy and propped my own pillows up behind me. The nurse handed Syria to me. I held her in the nook of my elbow and stared at her. Unannounced, Florence Nightingale grabbed my nipple and stuck it in Syria's mouth.

'Eina,' I screeched. Saying 'eina' hurt me more.

'Sorry mammie,' she smiled but kept tugging. Syria latched like a piranha. The thought of breastfeeding again, being trapped underneath a baby, made me sad. And angry. And frustrated. The nurse walked away and I caressed the side of my swollen breast with my free hand.

Lyle rested his hand on my shoulder and leaned in to whisper

189

in my ear, 'Stop going on like that. You a woman, your body is supposed to do this. Stop complaining. If I had a poes I would have had this laaitie myself.'

The whole time he spoke, he was smiling.

'I told Nadine I don't think it's gonna work with her. I wanna be with you and my laaitie,' he said in a more stern than romantic proposition. 'We have a child now, we must put this childish, fighting kak behind us.'

I didn't answer, but he had spoken and so it was by default almost. I just went through the motions. The post-birth hormones had not really allowed me any sort of rational, mental deliberation.

When I got home, I was in a daze. The pain in my abdomen was excruciating for the first week; but my family had made it very clear that this time around there would be no hiatus in my chores. I had arrived home from the hospital on Thursday and on that Sunday my mother told me to get up and make lunch.

I lifted myself up against the wall and used my arms to carry my weight against the tables and chairs and boxes in my room. I moved through the lounge to the kitchen and leaned heavily on the counters as I removed the food from the fridge and cupboards. I made it work, though. My left elbow leaned deeply into the counter supporting my weight and my right hand chopped onions, diced potatoes. The chicken roasted to perfection in the oven while the rice boiled. I didn't sit down once as I worked. I could do it, even through the pain. They needed to see that.

Syria's birth threw me back into the circular conflict that is an abusive romantic relationship. The thing about being with an abusive man is that the abuse is almost a fuel for you to leave. I would dare say that constant abuse is the best. A woman who is abused every single day, non-stop, is more likely to decide to run and never look back. It is those moments of calm, of bliss, that are the deadliest. Those deceitful moments are sirens, luring you into the loving, strong arms that caress you so well, so specifically – until the grip tightens, slowly. I have highlighted the monstrous parts of Lyle so that you can understand what he was capable of, but abusive men are charming, alluring. Lyle was the friendliest of friends, the sexiest of bachelors. He had no job or money, he had nothing to offer, but women flocked towards him. Good-looking, successful, smart women were willing to fight each other for a hit of that dopamine his acceptance released.

The first few weeks post birth were both calm and tumultuous. I had the luxury of Lyle coming and helping with the baby. He would hold her while I washed her. He dressed her and gave her a bottle. Having the baby's father there, equally responsible for the child's life felt good, it made me proud. We had two weeks of some sort of utopia that sunk me back into the vice grip. I could say things like, 'please clean the bottle while I change her nappy', or 'hold your laaitie for a second, I need to sit,' and it wouldn't be met with the usual rejection that I associated with having a los kind.

All of these things made the initial plan to leave so much more difficult. Having to weigh the balance between physical comfort and societal acceptance was a constant struggle.

I have to give myself credit for my awakening to the reality of who I had become. I couldn't live in denial anymore. I couldn't pretend I didn't notice the conditioning of myself and other Coloured women anymore. I grew tired of straightening my hair and rounding my Rs and biting my tongue so that I didn't anger people stupider than me. And the glaringly fragile masculinity of all the men around me started to choke me, even if they did nothing except stand in my presence.

Years of resentment, hiding my true nature and trying to be non-threatening was starting to fucking rip me apart. I couldn't be quiet for much longer.

But in the calmness, I couldn't break up with him. Everyone commented on how lucky I was, how attentive and helpful Lyle had become. I was the lucky one. But as I had expected, the calm exterior cracked, even sooner than I had anticipated. It started small, when I was alone with him and Syria one day midweek. He had come over to help and Sidney was at crèche. My father was at the hospital and my mom had gone to work. I opened the garage for Lyle and he came in, walking with that egotistical swagger that I hadn't seen in a while.

We went up the stairs to where Syria was sleeping. I hadn't bathed yet, because I was waiting for him to get there so that I could have some time in the bathroom without having to worry that she would woke up.

I made tea for him, cleaned and sterilised the bottles before getting my things to go shower.

'I'm horny; are we alone here?' He wasn't being aggressive, but my jaw and stomach tensed.

'No one is here. But I'm still bleeding.' That was a 'get out of rape free' card, or so I thought.

'Your mouth is mos oraait . . .'

So my mouth would do instead. He thought that was so clever.

I smiled and went to the bathroom. I climbed in the shower, still nervous. I was healing from the operation, so I wouldn't be able to put up much of a fight. I enjoyed the hot water rushing over my skin, washing off the sweat and blood of the last 24 hours. I was relieved that he hadn't climbed in with me, but then I realised that he was alone with Syria. My wound pulsated with pain. I turned to look through the crack in the door, to ease my anxiety. But I looked straight into Lyle's face, as he ejaculated at the bathroom door. In the moment, it relieved me that he chose to pleasure himself, even if it was at my expense. I didn't know that this violation of my personal space would be one of the nightmares that would follow me for years to come. I still don't like to shower, unless I am alone at home. I am scared to get soap in my eyes and open them to someone watching me, panting like a rabid dog.

I didn't make a thing of it and the day went on. The next time he visited it was evening time and everyone was home. A girl-friend of mine was visiting too. Again, the glint of the old Lyle showed in his eyes. It's hard to describe, but when abusive men are in one of their 'fragile' moods, their eyes have this glossed over quality that seems to be evolution's warning sign to the female partner to tread lightly.

My friend was talking to me, holding Syria, when Lyle said that he was horny. She knew about his shenanigans, but was being cordial for the sake of peace. My parents and Sidney were in the other room, so we both just smiled at him.

'She is mos here, we go downstairs,' he kept on. I kept my eyes down to avoid acknowledging what was happening.

'Must I talk louder?' He wasn't smiling anymore. If I didn't know any better, I would have said that he was being this way on purpose, in front of her. A show of dominance, peacocking. Or I guess, cocking.

'My parents are right here,' I giggled, again to pretend this was fine.

'So, they mos up here. We go downstairs. Sort me out,' he said and tapped my bum.

'How can you still ask?' My friend was openly agitated.

'I don't ask, I take,' Lyle retorted.

'What?' She was louder now.

'I don't ask, I take,' he gloated again.

She gritted her teeth and showed them and I interrupted the exchange. I touched her shoulder gently as I walked past, which she knew meant that I was coming back now.

'I am still bleeding.' I walked downstairs with him, but with no intention of having sex.

'We supposed to be back together and we still haven't had sex,' he said. He was serious.

I looked at him in bewilderment. 'I just had a baby.'

'Weeks ago.'

'Exactly, I am not allowed to have sex for like six weeks. And that is the minimum. I haven't healed yet,' I whispered, shouted.

'Who said so?' this ignoramus poes retorted.

'The doctor, Lyle.'

'Kak, he never said so to me. Come, it's your duty to keep me happy. I have been helping the whole time with this laaitie,' he said, unbuckling.

'Please don't talk so loud.' I walked to the door and closed it. 'My mother is going to start looking for me soon. I am going back upstairs.'

'Must I tell you sexed me in the garage when you were pregnant?'

'What?'

'You heard me. Or you can just let me put it in, gou.'

I stood in limbo, hearing myself heave. I wanted to scream, but I couldn't put my parents through another round of this.

I pulled down my maternity jeans and stood against the built-in cupboards. I smelled the menstrual blood unplug with each thrust. He was gentle, though. The one time I didn't want him to go slow, he relished in my post-birth mess. It didn't feel like I had skin down there. He was moving his shaft against an inner layer of my body. A part that wasn't supposed to be touched.

'Please make it quick,' I whispered in broken cadence. He came inside of me. I would later find the cum, mixed with my blood, like a tiedye on my panty. The visual made me cry silently in the bathroom, on my knees on the cold tiles to better muffle the sounds.

When I tell you I was broken, in pieces, I meant it in every way.

That was the last time we had sex. But that wasn't why I left him for good.

The day that catapulted me into the decision to leave for good was the afternoon he asked me to give my son away.

Friends of ours, a couple, had come to visit and help me with the baby. Lyle sat on the bed with Syria-Rose, while I prepared the bathwater. My friends were in the dining room, playing with Sidney. Sidney walked past the door a few times and watched for a few seconds as Lyle, Syria and I went about our lives as a family. I didn't realise it at the time, but at four years old, he already knew that the man with me was his sister's father, but wasn't his. I never considered what that must feel like for a child. It must have been so confusing.

Lyle must have seen him too, before Sidney walked back to my friends.

After a few seconds, Lyle asked me, quietly, 'Why don't you give him to them? They really love him.'

I didn't respond immediately; not out loud nor in my head. My mind resounded with silence, my brain stilled. I realised I had taken a real glimpse into this man's head. I had had a no-holds-barred peek into the darkness of his soul.

195

To him, we were our own family and he didn't want the responsibility of caring for another man's child. His pride in his family came from the fact that his seed had created it. I can see that to the unaccomplished man, virility can become a measuring stick of success. My son was also evidence that I had had a sex life before our relationship and it was getting in the way of his picture-perfect family.

I will be embarrassingly honest: for a second I was torn. Everything I had learned about the conventional family up until this point told me that his feelings about my 'los kind' were expected and valid. My community had long normalised the abandonment of ''n ander man se kind'.

Children required responsibility and money. I had myself been dehumanised as a child by only being there to toe a line. And all of this made me feel very, very angry at myself. And then, I felt anger towards my son. I felt angry at my child for being born and potentially destroying my happily ever after. For a second, I was inside of the situation, about to be manipulated by this 'man'. But I promise you, it was a very, very short second. That moment was the catalyst for change. Something in my mind said 'no'. I heard it, audibly. As if someone next to me said it. Someone external from my many levels of consciousness. I looked at Lyle as he waited for me to say something. He didn't even have the decency to make eye contact with me while asking me to abandon my child. He kept his eyes on our daughter. His daughter.

Finally, I managed a simple, 'He's my son,' to which he replied a nonchalant, 'I'm joking, man. Just wanted to see what you gonna say.'

But he wasn't joking.

Deep inside, I knew that this wasn't how people were supposed to treat other people; no matter how badly that person's past played out, surely there was no justification for outright cruelty. Up until that point I had stayed and whenever I left, I would return, making excuses. I believed that because I had veered so far from the path of chastity and had had babies, I needed to latch on to this man. I honestly thought that as I matured, I would be able to handle my abusive boyfriend, my son who didn't have a father, my infant daughter – and that the whole experience would make me stronger. Because women are supposed to suffer and get stronger, right? That's how it works? It was what I had seen the ladies in my family do. All of my uncles were abusive. I'd seen it in Christian movies. Surely if I just married him and then prayed for him in a dedicated prayer closet and sexed him whenever he needed me to be his rock, then he would be a good man in return?

Nah. I could feel that bitch was gone. Now, every time he did something I went to the cops, He had directly threatened my son and something inside of me believed him. If he could beat me like that, what could he do to a four-year-old?

Okay, it wasn't that easy.

I told him to leave me alone and I went to court to make a case. Then I dropped it. And I made another case. And I dropped it. And so it went for a few months, until I just stopped. I stopped responding to him, I stopped missing him. But this time, I wasn't even convinced by my periodical 'new-found strength', that seemed to dissipate whenever Lyle offered me affection.

I fought myself. I fought myself hard. I needed accountability more than my own word.

And then in my loneliest and most confused moment, I sat down at my parents' dining room table and looked over the entirety of Pelican Heights, onto the Strandfontein ocean – and used the only marketable skill I had. I wrote. For no one. For myself. I wrote a short blog about having my card declined while buying milk. I just needed to vent. I didn't have friends to lose. I didn't have anyone's respect to lose. There was a long battle with myself about what was appropriate to write about. A push-pull between what was embarrassing, what made me sound good, what was true. The line between authenticity and self-deprecation became thinner the more I delved deeper into what was really happening and into who I really was. And when I posted it, I remember closing my laptop and going to the park next to my house with my children. I sat there and watched Sidney play and held Syria on my lap. And I cried. Not wildly, or dramatically. I just sat there as the tears streamed down my face as Sidney, oblivious to the failure his mother was, played happily on the merry-go-round. I didn't know it yet, but that day my life would do a 180. But I was now alone again, unemployed and broke. The world was laughing at me already, so I may as well have controlled what they laughed at.

In January 2015, I got a job in journalism. After four years as a qualified journalist, all I could get was a junior position for half of what I had previously earned. R6000. That was the salary on offer. It was a start-up and they needed someone immediately. I swallowed my pride and took it. The boss at the time, Tony Seifart, was the first white man in my industry (and in the world, actually) to ever show me kindness. He knew my story and kept me onboard through the many phases of healing that would happen over the next few years. He upped my salary pretty quickly and in finding this new career, I made friends who kept me solid in my resolve to not go back to Lyle. There, I worked with two women who were more fixated on the success of the team than their own petty bullshit. And I was part of the team. They taught me words and how to do news. They gave me a reason to get up each day and come in to a real job. I was humbled very quickly by how little I knew. I was so depressed at that time that I didn't even get dressed for work at first. I went to the office in pajamas, or broken pants. They kept pushing me. Through it, I blogged. It kept me accountable. If I told the world about how Lyle would beat me and rape me when I was with him then I couldn't just go back when it got hard.

After six months, the colour came back into my face. I had a routine, a new wardrobe. Every day I would get up, get the kids ready and take them to crèche. I drove to work. After work I would go down to the Spar below the office and get some snacks for the kids and I and go home, happy to see them. It sounds trivial, but I was happy to see my children and I could get them treats and make them smile when they saw me. No one had ever smiled when they saw me before.

I had taken Lyle to maintenance court, but they didn't really come through for me. Maintenance court is another bane of the Coloured female existence. The whole maintenance system is based on the premise that if you have a baby with a man and you aren't married to him, you have to assume all of the parenting responsibility and he is allowed to contribute whatever is comfortable for him.

If you're married when you have his child and you get divorced, you have to assume all of the parenting responsibility and he can get the kids every second weekend and contribute what is comfortable for him.

If the kids cost on average R10 000 a month, your whole salary goes for their upbringing and he can contribute what is comfortable for him each month. Which will be calculated by a group of men, in a court of law.

If you are married and stay together, you have to take on all of the responsibility of taking care of the kids and he is allowed to offer what is comfortable for him.

The whole system is based on the comfort of men and the discomfort of the women who don't want them in their lives anymore.

You get it.

Lyle gave me R500 every two weeks for Syria, then asked me to give him a R50 back to travel home. I quickly learned not to add his contribution to my budget. Independence felt better than arguing with a moron over a bag of nappies' worth of money. My independence brought an awakening. The more things I chose to do for myself, the less ill-treatment I was willing to tolerate from anyone.

On the Sunday of Lyle's weekend in August 2015, I fetched Syria from his house. I had come from a friend and was dressed up. I stopped outside and let him put Syria in the car. I didn't go inside. We weren't friends at this point and I wanted to get my child and go home. I pulled up and knocked on the door. Lyle emerged, a little tipsy. I had noticed the unfamiliar car parked in front of his house. His friends were there, chilling in the entertainment section of his garage.

'Don't go yet, I wanna chat to you,' he said. I rolled my eyes. His attempts at speaking to me had become exasperating. He found a way to speak to me as much as he could even while he enjoyed telling people I was obsessed with him. I tolerated him at this point. I still loved him, but I was starting to love myself more.

'Yes Lyle?'

'You look lekker ne? Don't wear that bra when you come here,' he laughed. He looked behind him. His new girlfriend, not Nadine, was in the house.

I laughed, but not from shyness. Poor bitch.

'You look lekker, yoh. You and my daughter are kak beautiful.'
I got into the car.

'Roll down the window,' he mouthed as I pulled out, slowly. A few weeks prior I had finally taken the step of getting a restraining order against him. I had fetched Syria after one of his weekends, when he had pulled the same stunt, trying to talk to me. But when he handed her over, he whispered to me: 'Yoh, her poes look just like yours. While I was changing her nappy I soema got a houte.'

I still cannot quite believe that he told me our daughter gave him a hard-on. I went straight to the police station, but they said that all I could do was make a case and get a restraining order. They couldn't do anything about his visitation rights, though. Only the maintenance court could do that. We had an appointment for a revision on the 7th of September. Which meant that he still had a few visits before then and if I didn't send her, I would go to jail.

So when I fetched her that last day in August, I only tolerated him to keep us both safe. I drove away and breathed a sigh of relief that there were a whole two weeks between that moment and seeing Lyle again. I was going to tell the court everything when we appeared. I wasn't going to drop the case this time.

In September 2015 I was happy. My career was starting to blossom, my blog was gaining popularity. I had a job and I had a purpose. I had a plan. Nothing was going to throw me off my game anymore.

On the 5th of September 2015 I woke up to a message from Lyle's mother: 'Hi Shana. I just wanted to let you know that Lyle was murdered last night.'

Fuck.

# Chapter 12

# Death becomes her

One of the most emotionally significant moments of my life was finding out that my abuser had died. He hadn't just died; my fantasy had crossed the line into being a reality. That worthless, evil motherfucker was murdered as he deserved, or so my initial anger and simultaneous gratitude surmised in the throes of actual, devastating grief.

To be clear, I don't think I was ever sad that Lyle was dead. Not for that fact alone, anyways. If I was sad about anything surrounding his death, it was for the part of me that still held onto the fantasy that we would have ended up together. One day. Perhaps in decades, our unrequited love would have prevailed and we would have been grown and mature enough to laugh at our silly mistakes from our youth. It was a nonsense thought, but the fantasy gave me strength to leave, somehow. A belief that it wasn't the end. That I hadn't abandoned him but asserted myself.

When he died, I felt guilt so severe that I blamed myself for his death for a long time. As if I had willed it into reality somehow, by wanting him out of my life. It really did feel like a karmic gift, personally sent to me by an external, other-worldly force. Like I had made a deal with the devil. Still, I have never wished that anything had happened differently on that September morning.

On 4 September, Lyle went out drinking with his father, a well-known gangster on the Cape Flats. Lyle's friends were with him and they apparently went all over the peninsula that night, between Mitchell's Plain and Bayview, eventually ending up at a merchant's home in Strandfontein's old village. Interestingly, Lyle's biological uncle had been murdered at that same smokkie a few days prior. He had called me during the week to speak about it, although I hadn't been interested in picking up.

'I am at work, Lyle,' I answered the phone, annoyed at his audacity.

He said something about us making amends and having supper some time. I half-listened, fully emersed in my job and proud to be.

'Boney died.'

'Okay, when are you gonna vrek?' I really said that to him.

'Yoh, you really want me to die?'

He sounded genuinely astounded. I didn't understand how he didn't understand that I hated him. After everything, he didn't see how it was possible. A fascinating insight into the psychology of abusers. Devoid of accountability. The true victims of their actions.

'I do.'

'Kak heavy,' he laughed and spoke some more, but I cut him off.

'I am at work, Lyle, and the restraining order is supposed to be with you already. Please only message me about Syria.'

I put down. Other irrelevant things were said but that conversation has faded in my memory over the years. Everything he ever said to me had become less significant or clear in my mind the more my life changed. The good things, anyway.

I went about my workday thinking about how different he had sounded on the phone. He had a new type of calmness, an energy that wasn't aggressive, that I had never felt from him before. It didn't even feel like the Lyle I knew was talking.

He called me again that night again to say one thing, 'Hi, Shana. The restraining order came now. Yoh.' Silence.

'Yep,' I said, proud of myself. As I should have been.

'Okay.'

'Okay.'

'Bye, Shana.'

'Bye, Lyle.'

He hung up. That was the last conversation we had.

That night, I had a dream. I was standing at AFDA and I was nervous. Lyle, the old Lyle that I had lived with, was coming for me. He was chasing me. I spotted him and saw that his eyes were wild, demonic. I ran up a flight of stairs that led outside to a metal balcony and as I got to the precipice, I felt his body touch mine from behind. He grabbed my mouth and we looked down to the ground. It was so far down. Rubble, weeds, broken bricks, blocks of cement and other dirt. He jumped with me though, still keeping my mouth closed. We free-fell for a while until I felt the earth on my face. We had landed hard, protected only by the fuzziness of the dream world. I remember being amazed that I was unscathed. I stood up, free from his grip. In the distance there were women standing in a doorway. They were sisters, I knew. They wore black dresses. They said, 'She can see us. Come.' I recognised the woman from the side of the road from the night I had met Lyle. Lyle. I turned back to see if he was okay. But when I looked back, he was lying dead in the rubble; and I lay there too, a version of me, dead in his arms.

That Friday I went to work and came home as normal. Syria was already sleeping when I got home around 5ish. That was pretty odd for her, a very active, sleep-avoiding one-year-old. I took my small mercy and got into bed with Siddo. He fell asleep too and I put on a movie: *Room 1308*. I dozed off pretty quickly, lekker relaxed, ready for the weekend.

When I woke up to a phone full of notifications, I had no idea what was happening.

Those days, I was used to having my phone blow up because of Facebook and my blog, so I didn't think anything was up. As I was about to open the app, my phone rang.

'Babes, are you okay?' my friend Philly asked me.

'Yes, babes, why?'

'Is Lyle really dead?' she asked.

'Hey?' I think I laughed, I can't be sure.

'I am not sure. I have a lot of messages. Can I phone you back?'

I put down the phone and opened Facebook, straight onto a picture of him, a tribute by one of his friends. I didn't scroll. I just looked. I felt fokkol. It wasn't real. Not yet.

I went into my messages. That is when I saw the text from his mom.

Apparently, when he had been dropped at home that Saturday morning around 3am, he had told his friends that he wanted to sit and smoke a cigarette on the porch before he went inside.

The neighbourhood watch had seen a car stop there shortly after and he went willingly to the vehicle. They assumed he knew the people. He got into the car and then ran away to the field behind his house. It is assumed he was going to try to jump the wall. But he had been stabbed in the heart. The mixture of his blood alcohol level and his racing heart made him bleed out in seconds. He collapsed dead at the wall. Amidst the rubble and broken bricks and sand.

The day dragged. I was in a strange limbo, a bubble of sorts. I wasn't sure yet how I felt. Was I happy with my newfound freedom? What did everyone expect me to feel? Happiness at someone's death is distasteful, although when Hitler died, I doubt anyone defended him. I was very confused about what was appropriate and what was real. Perhaps logging onto social media wasn't the best idea. I was immediately bombarded by tributes to the son of a bitch. Just pages and pages of people who never even saw him since high school and posts about how he always had a smile.

That afternoon I took Syria to his mom's home to pay my respects. His family and the church members we both had grown up in front of were there. I walked into the lounge and said good afternoon. No one responded. I didn't expect them to. I was the pariah. A traitor. The person who reported him to the police before he died. The person who wrote of his private shenanigans in my detestable blog.

I sat there in the silence for a while out of reverence and tradition. Then I left Syria there on her grandmother's request. I went home and lay down in the silence of a Lyle-less world. I got into bed and the tears streamed, but calmly. I wasn't crying, just tearing. I put my face into a pillow and fell into a headachey half sleep. Later that day, I made my way to Lyle's night vigil, alone. My friends had all refused to join me out of principle. The fact that I needed them there to support me, instead of honour him, was lost on them. The vigil was a blur. It was a whole road filled with people who didn't know Lyle. They stared at me as I walked to the house. I heard them whisper about how I reported him for things he did not do (or things they saw him do but disassociated from his personality).

When I got home that night, I sat in silence. I couldn't hear myself through my thoughts. I sat down at my laptop and wrote a tribute to Lyle. To our lives that had been and would never be.

I romanticised the struggle for love that had engulfed me since the day I was born and culminated in my relationship with Lyle. I used every emotion-provoking literary device as I wrote that piece. I don't even know why I wrote it. Part of me wanted to prove to everyone who thought I was the bad guy that I did love Lyle. I think I tried to prove to myself that I didn't feel happy that he was dead. I needed to feel human. That post was shared over 5000 times that night. A post of lies, I told myself, forever immortalised as my best work. Giving the people what they wanted always went viral. No one really cares about the truth, just what feels good.

When I woke up for work on Monday morning, I couldn't speak. My throat had full-on closed. My tonsils were inflamed, rendering me speechless. The irony isn't lost on me. I could feel Lyle's hand still wrapped firmly around my lips. I didn't speak for a week. Syria stayed by her ma for that next week.

I also wasn't allowed to attend the funeral. Well, perhaps 'not allowed' is a strong term, but I certainly wasn't welcomed. So, out of respect for his mother and because I am a fucking coward who has been traumatised to the point of hating any face-to-face confrontation, I stayed home.

The aftermath of Lyle's death was the start of a new phase in my mental suffering. I was now in the stage of my life in which my dreams were actualising and honestly, for someone who never felt worthy of any sort of success, the pressure to not fuck this up was so extreme that I was more of a mess than when I was unsuccessful. After Lyle died, I had no more excuses. I worked seven days a week, 20 hours a day. I was the actual definition of a single mother.

I also denounced any future romantic relationships. I saw any sort of sexuality or fraternising as the enemy. Two months down the line I was the editor of the newsroom, earning double what I used to and full swing into the egotistical side of feminism. I didn't need a man, I was a man. Yes, that is a problematic statement, but it is the mindset I adapted as a coping mechanism for the chaos and loneliness that consumed me when I was supposed to be happy and grateful to God for giving me another chance. Unworthy me, who had only made mistakes for 25 years. Me, the sexually deviant, spoiled mother of two illegitimate children from two different men; I was delivered from evil and now the world's eyes were on me.

In this transitional period, my dad sold our childhood home and I felt as if life as I knew it was being ripped away in every corner. I couldn't stop imagining an unreal, angelic version of Lyle and I missed him. Lyle the saint – the way one remembers the dead is the same way one remembers giving birth. Only the good part. It's what allows you to have another baby and put yourself through all of that shit again. I guess one could argue that the brain does the same thing when leaving an abuser. I couldn't go back to him this time though; there were no trains to hell.

Still, I was soon giving myself over to the motions of my new life. I would be remiss to say it was all bad. I was actually very proud of myself. I felt powerful in my new role. And for good measure, the pressure and fast pace of the business had made me lekker thin. My parents and I were on good terms for the first time ever, I was wearing normal people clothes, brushing my hair and most importantly, I wasn't pregnant.

And here, in this space, my husband found me.

One day at work, I checked in on an old friend on Facebook Messenger, just to shoot the breeze as we had always done in intervals for five years.

Riyaahd Fife, one of the few men I knew who had a good job and was kind and level-headed. So of course, I didn't smaak him in the slightest. We chatted briefly and the next day, he said hello again.

It turned out that he worked down the road from me, so we planned to grab a coffee and chat properly. I wasn't nervous at all and actually welcomed the embrace of a familiar, safe, platonic conversation. I hadn't seen anyone in real life in so long. I had no idea that when Riyaahd and I made eye contact while grabbing that coffee I would never want to look anywhere else ever again.

We spent the rest of the summer of 2015 just pretending to be platonic, but stealing moments at Canal Walk, or at events. We pretended to be interested in hooking each other up with people we knew. Every day I would get a good morning text and we spoke all day until I voice-noted a sleepy 'goodnight'. One night, after a particularly boring comedy show, we sat in my car, chatting as we always did to stall going home.

'Do we like each other?"' he asked me.

The conversation had finally gotten there. We both laughed at the idea that there could be something romantic between us.

'We are friends,' I said and he concurred. We both honestly believed, from our experiences with less than stellar partners over the years, that romance was the end of happy friendships. It is funny how most people believe that these two relationship types should be separated.

'But perhaps we should kiss?'

We had the whole Schrödinger's cat conversation and in the opposite of a lapse in judgement, we kissed each other. As friends. With tongue. He tasted like beer. I resisted the urge to mount him in the parking lot of Premium Sports Bar. We sat back and giggled at our own childishness. But we had crossed a line, levelled up somehow. I dropped him at home and acted nonchalant. I was actually elated and terrified. I knew that once boys and girls got physical, things changed. My vagina was excited, but my brain could have honestly grounded her for life.

I went to bed that night very nervous that he would never speak to me again.

I saw my text when I got into bed.

'You home already?'

I didn't brush my teeth that night. I could still smell his cologne on my face. Beer and Chanel Blue for men. A far cry from the Axe-wearing naaiers I was used to.

We remained friends for a few more days, until he kissed me again, unexpectedly . . . but I didn't act as cool this time. When his lips touched mine, I actually felt those butterflies I had always pretended I felt before. It scared me.

'Please get out,' I asked him as politely as I could. He exited my car, confused, and I sped away at a speed I didn't even know my low-powered car could do. As I drove, I cried. I couldn't even see the road clearly. I was fucking my life up again. I envisioned my next solo pregnancy and I knew that this time the failure of the relationship would hurt more. It was too perfect.

I also felt like I was being served my happy ending, but I was too chickenshit to claim it.

But then again, we all know that fairytales don't exist.

When I got home, I sat on the bathroom floor and messaged him.

'Sorry about that. I understand if you don't want to see me anymore'. I put my phone in my pocket and tried to forget about him. I didn't realise just how dramatic I was being until years later.

'You need to calm down,' was his take on things. I was offend-ed, affronted by the truth. We spoke about how I wasn't ready to trust someone, or be in love. I felt naked, exposed by having to have conversations about my feelings. When we decided that we weren't going to go back to being just friends, the fear of tell-ing people ate me up inside. I knew that telling my family that I had a boyfriend would anger them. My mother didn't even want to meet Riyaahd at first.

'Hy kommie hier nie, he can't come here,' she insisted, obvi-ously traumatised by my past: but who wasn't at this point? I had to go as far as to assure her that he was saved and that we weren't having sex. In accordance with Christianity and society's need to police my vagina, which was apparently still on parole.

We got married. After a year. And yes, it may have been a mistake.

Don't get me wrong, my husband and I are still wildly in love, but love isn't all that relationships take and after a year, you haven't even cracked the surface of who your partner is and what the fuck is wrong with them. The rosy exterior of our whirlwind romance remained in the world-facing forefront, but underneath we were in trouble – real trouble.

But not in the way you would expect.

Abuse can affect the abused in various ways. Some survivors go on to heal the world, some turn into monsters and serial kill-ers. We hardly speak about the survivors who end up having to continue life somewhere in the middle.

Survivor. I really hate that world. I personally see it as a word that makes others feel better. It gives the impression that abuse or trauma is but one event that one can come out of, unscathed, on the other side. But to this day, I am still dealing with the trauma and how everything that happened to me has impacted my life. So have I survived it in the true sense of the word? I resonate more with 'casualty', 'experiencer'.

I started to notice certain things about myself fairly quickly into my marriage. I was with a new man, yet I expected the previous man's behaviour to rear its head at any second and so I found myself on the offensive more often than I would like to admit. I was uncomfortable in my happiness. I didn't know how to navigate a healthy home. There was no danger lurking around every corner. I could stay up as late as I wanted. I could sleep in if I so desired; which I never have because the thought makes me feel lazy. (Rest makes me feel like a failure. I only feel okay when I am working towards a goal; even if the goal is small, or irrelevant in the greater scheme of things, being idle makes me feel deviant, sleg.)

'What are you doing on your phone?' I would ask Riyaahd when he checked messages or just scrolled. I just knew that when he wasn't focused on me, he was talking to women. Nothing else made sense. In the beginning he would just casually turn his phone to show me his screen. I had all his passcodes and the freedom to pry whenever the anxiety made the monster who lived in my chest flare up, but I knew that it wasn't fair on him.

When we would argue, the same thing would happen. Fully cognizant of the fact that I wasn't in an abusive relationship, the slightest provocation or disagreement would launch me into fight mode. I both had control over and didn't have control over myself and my reactions. I didn't understand how I could get so very, very angry and ready to fight when I wasn't even in danger. My body was so used to being defensive that I was now the one who wouldn't listen to reason. But honestly, if anyone tried to reason with me it would feel like lies; they were tricking me so that they could hurt me. Being abused, humiliated and so many other things had skewed my perception. And it was eating away at my marriage.

We argued almost daily at one point. We were both happy and frustrated at the same time. When it was good, it was good for weeks. But anytime we had to deal with anything that I thought impeded on my personal freedoms, like budgeting or things that needed attention around the house, I sort of exited my body in anger.

'Don't take me for a poes, jou naai,' I would get aggressive. I felt like a rottweiler on a leash. The leash was merely the loose fingered grip that I still had on reality. I was letting go though and I couldn't find my way back to normal. I was making up for lost time, making the transition from timid victim into someone who needed to call out everything, to fight about anything. Sometimes I felt anger radiate through my body like a physical entity.

I kept promising that I would fix my anger issues and seek help. I had already had a very deep bipolar episode in our relationship and Riyaahd had chosen to navigate that particular storm with me, no matter how many dramatic 'you don't deserve this' speeches I gave him through snot and tears. I knew in my soul he deserved a whole person. He also didn't have kids or baggage like mine and I was aware of what his family and friends thought of his choice to hitch his wagon to a single mother of multiple successful sperms. Even I was suspicious of his intentions. But he had been solid in his resolve, a personality trait that I both love and despise about my husband.

The coup de grâce was when I swung my claws at him in a fit of rage one morning before work. My nail caught his eyeball and he fell back into the wall, grabbing his face. I was so angry that I didn't even stop to check if he was okay. I said something along the lines of him deserving it and I stormed out. That is the day I realised that I needed help.

I went back on medication and promised myself that I would never raise my hands to my husband or my children again.

But that wasn't the only side effect of the abuse. I couldn't have sex.

This was a challenge I hadn't expected to face.

I waited for years to know the guilt-free pleasure of having sex within the constraints of marriage. I always thought that I was an expert at it. I had been having it since my teens and men always ejaculated theatrically. Surely that was the only purpose. Apparently not. My husband had ideas of his own. Female pleasure, a concept completely foreign to me until that point.

The first time we had sex, I didn't notice it. The second time neither. But at some point, I caught myself counting in my head, while we did it.

Literally, I would go '1, 2, 3, 4, 5, 6, 7 . . .' and so on, purposefully taking my mind away from the action. I couldn't explain it but every time we started anything sexual I would disassociate, or distract myself with delusion.

Sometimes, when he would enter me, I would imagine fantastical scenarios like I was rolling in a barrel, or on a sinking ship. And through the thrusts, I would pretend I wasn't there.

My nipples were a no-go zone. When he kissed them, I would get angry. I felt dirty. All I could think about was Lyle sucking them wildy and calling me Mommy. My body could remember every violation. Wherever Riyaahd would touch me, that part of my body would release a memory, or a suppressed feeling. Even if I consciously tried to relax my body, any stimulation that felt good even for a few seconds, like rubbing my clitoris against him, would launch me into fits of sobbing.

I felt so guilty: I kept relapsing into the five-year-old girl who was caught pleasuring herself on that couch. Arousal catapulted me into that memory, every time. The last time I felt pleasure before the abuse, mos.

Outside my bedroom, many women revered me as if I really was a fucking survivor. I felt like a fraud. But opening my mouth about my struggle would diminish their hope that they too could be happy one day.

I would be lying if I said this has been resolved. It has certainly improved, but there is a very long journey ahead of me.

When we had pretty much settled into the rollercoaster that is marriage, I fell pregnant. I had always imagined that this moment would be happy if I were married and secure. I chased that same high in my last two pregnancies. I remember distinctly how I tried to imagine that I was married when I had them both in my tummy. I would lie in bed and close my eyes and just picture what it felt like to be going through pregnancy married.

I had been feeling that familiar nauseous feeling and one Saturday, I sent Riyaahd to get some groceries, a bottle of red wine and a pregnancy test. I didn't even think I was really pregnant. I didn't want to believe that nonsense. It wasn't exactly a pleasant memory for me.

I poured myself a dop and sat down on the toilet. Pissed my hand wet while I aimed for the test. I left the test on the toilet and went to the kitchen to have a drink with Riyaahd as we waited for a negative result.

I couldn't take a sip, though. I was too nervous. Riyaahd fetched it and I looked. The two lines made me cry. I walked to the room sans alcohol and I lay on the bed.

Riyaahd stood in front of me, smiling.

'Why are you so happy?' I asked him.

'We gonna have another baby,' he said. 'Why wouldn't I be happy?'

And that was when I knew I was going to be okay. He had counted this baby as number three, not as number one. He pulled me up by my one hand and hugged me. I didn't know if he was being ironic or sincere. This level of affection was making me uncomfortable and I wanted to laugh at it. He still held on to me though. I cried for a while. He tucked me in and I just spent the rest of the day reeling.

I kept having to remind myself that it was okay. He couldn't leave me, legally. I picked up my phone and messaged my mom and sister in the family WhatsApp group.

'I want to tell you guys something,' I dipped my toe in. I was genuinely nervous.

'Jy's pregnant?' My mother didn't care much for showmanship.

'Yes,' I said.

'Is that a good idea?' my sister chimed in.

And that was it. Fears confirmed that my uterus would never bring honour. It was forever known by its bad decisions.

But things got better fairly quickly. My dad drove to me the next day and said congratulations and that I mustn't worry about what my mom and sister say. I was married and my husband wanted a baby: to my dad, this was the right way. It gave me solace.

My children also met the news with great excitement. It soon started the girls against boys split in my house. Girls are in the lead, always. The pregnancy went pretty quickly. I was in some-one else's world. I could sit in bed and have someone else do my chores now. I had license to crave things and the money to buy those same things, which was a serious fucking trip. Everyone was so nice to me. I was plunged into a real-life version of the dream world I had lived in in my head during the first two pregnancies.

My mother had come round too. She would say things like, 'Moeti soe baie staani my kind, jy moet rus'. Hearing her telling me to sit to rest, to take care of myself, was very far from her earlier attitude and helped make me feel my life had truly changed.

When we walked into our appointments, Riyaahd would carry my bag. He opened the door for me and before I sat down, he would clear my chair. It was pretty extra and I wanted it to be. It was always about a ten-minute wait for our appointment, so we would sit and hold hands and talk about what the baby's name would be and whether it was a boy or a girl.

One time the kids went with us and he watched them while I was just sitting there, being pregnant.

The first time we heard her heartbeat, we both cried, just a little. Riyaahd held my hand and took a video of the sound coming out from the machine.

He didn't even swear at me once.

# Epilogue

If this was a Hallmark movie, my story would end there, in sort of a full, circular narrative that would leave you all warm and fuzzy at how everything always works out in the end. But my life in the last few years since my third pregnancy hasn't been a walk in the park – not entirely. Like I mentioned earlier, my marriage and 'happy ending' can be more honestly described as the beginning of a very painful healing process – plus, it is hard to ignore the fact that as I write this memoir of my many traumas, I am stuck in my home in the midst of a global pandemic.

After the birth of my third child, Scarlett-Grey, I was mostly okay. I experienced some sad days, but nothing near the darkness that came with previous post-partem periods. The main difference was that I wasn't alone. Riyaahd would usually wake up with me in the evening and was hands-on with Scarlett when I needed to spend time with the other two kids. And when she only wanted me, he would be with Sidney and Syria.

But again, my anxiety reared its ugly head. The trauma comes in waves. I couldn't shake the thought that he loved his biological child more. I kept seeing Sidney walk past the door when Lyle and I bathed Syria. I had blocked the memory out for so long, because I never had the time to deal with it. But now, I wasn't able to look away from the pain so easily anymore.

I suppose, for women like me, there will always be that fear that the man you are with prefers his biological kid. That is the price of the blended family. If the feelings aren't real, or the bond isn't forged early, there isn't really a thread to tie your loyalties together. For the parent in the middle, that can be devastating. I thought often of how my aunty had to make a choice to leave her 'outside child' at my ma's house so that she could have a husband and nuclear family under his roof. I felt responsible for not allowing that spirit of exclusivity to rest on my family, like the generational curse it was (and other nonsense thoughts).

But I trudged through the self-doubt and fear of embarrassment one day at a time and when the big kaboom didn't come, I started to actually believe that my life was in fact fine.

It's important that I note that it wasn't fine because I am married. One can be fine without any of the conventions society has put into place. Marriage is not a saviour or an absolver. In fact, marriage is an example of an institution that is pretending it isn't patriarchal by its very nature. (It's just about liberated women, waiting for the man to decide when it is time to get serious.) As long as we have the 'men only propose' version of marriage that we hold so dear – until we change it to a mutual conversation that can be brought up by the female part of the hetero-relationship without the judgement that she must be racing her biological clock – we have made zero real strides. Do not tell me we are equal, but then also say that marriage doesn't count as romantic when initiated by women. We can't have both.

But I've noticed that anyone who is on my side of this discussion is always accused of wanting to destroy the wholesomeness of the nuclear family, as if getting controlled by a man is some sort of blessing from God. Strap on those strap-ons, bitches, we have a long fight ahead of us.

I digress. My life is fine now because I am safe. I have never been safe before. Not with my body. Not with my emotions or thoughts.

Once I accepted that I was safe, my family of five soon found its rhythm. Something changed in me. I could feel a maternal energy growing inside of me, stirring, and suddenly as if I had always been this way, I was waking up at 4am, making sandwiches, cleaning the house and making nutritional suppers amidst chauffeuring the children to school and sports practice and preparing family braais and doing activities with the children; painting, making slime.

For the first time in my whole life, I enjoyed being at home.

I noticed that I didn't make excuses to get away from Scarlett, even though she was a baby. I wasn't annoyed by her neediness, as I had been before with my other kids. I enjoyed her phases, instead of dreading them because I would need to handle her alone.

My new circumstances and having that unspoken co-sign from society that allowed me to wear my tired mommyness openly on my face was strange. I was allowed to exist in my narrative without shame merely because a man had validated me as 'still good enough'. Soon, when the high wore off, I didn't want this privilege. I had seen the other side from the trenches. I was, am, still an outsider in my head and in my heart. I am a perpetual single mother, at my core. I couldn't just accept my new place at the table, when other moms were being treated like garbage.

And then, PTSD struck again.

*National Headline: Gender-based Violence Incidents up by 80% in SA Lockdown*

Another wave of trauma – though this headline news turned out to be inaccurate – and then disgust at myself for fucking making everything about me. In the lockdown, I was self-indulgent for more days than I like to admit. Me, with my first world problems, I was launched into my personal equivalent of a Vietnam flashback: trapped in a house again, with rules and regulations on where I could go and what I could do. You may as well have put me back into that separate entrance with Lyle.

Trauma aside, which is apparently something I am able to put aside now, nothing showed me the inequality that exists between penis-having and vagina-having human beings than the great equaliser, the lockdown. Men and women of the working class reacted differently to the announcement.

A common theme in my household and households like mine was that the women were tired, but the men seem revitalised by the impromptu holiday that none of us asked for.

My day and, from research, the days of my fellow women in arms went as follows: Wake up at 4am. Finish some work and take a shower before the children awake from their undeserved, delicious slumber.

They're awake early, fuck that shower, make breakfast. There is no rest for the fertile. Feed everyone. Facilitate potty time. Clean. Start facilitating homeschool lessons - and prepare snacks while you speak to your own, male boss on the phone through your earphones, praying he can't hear the viennas sizzling in the pan as you waffle about work you honestly looked at through one eye because of how exhausted you are.

After lunch, make your older kid watch the baby while you poop and then shower, both with the door open, as to not completely abandon them for even a minute in case they die and everyone blames your negligence. Explain for the hundredth time why the passage now smells like poop.

Get dressed with only 40 seconds to spare before your Zoom

meeting starts and smile through the meeting, pretending you're wearing a full outfit instead of a blazer, a shirt and your husband's boxer shorts. Mute yourself for the whole thing, so that no one can hear Peppa Pig being a bit of a bitch to daddy pig – honestly, she's awful.

Once the Zoom ends, make supper. Feed everyone. Clean up. Bath the kids. Put them to bed. Make a cup of coffee and sit down at your laptop to finish the work you started ambitiously at 4am. Work for a few hours and get into bed. Have sex with your husband, because shame, he does so much. Watch a few videos while he sleeps. Revel in the silence. Drift off and skrik awake when your alarm goes off at 4am. Surprise bitch, it's Groundhog Day.

Men's days went a lot like my husband's: wake up at 5 to 8, to start work at 8. Switch on computer. Fart. Receive coffee from gorgeous wife. Close the door, only to emerge for lunch and then return to the room and close the door again until after work, at 4.30pm.

Get supper served to you. Ask if your wife needs help with anything and pretend you didn't know the 'No' she said was sarcastic. Pat yourself on the back for cleaning the kitchen sometimes. Rock your wife's world with your magnificent cock and fall asleep cradling her buttocks and bosom. Think about how blessed you are to have found each other as you fall asleep.

In this PTSD bubble, the bad dreams had me by the throat ever since week 1. It was mostly the same every night. I would be at some or other event at my childhood home and Lyle would be waiting outside for me to hurry up and get done. The anxiety was palpable. It always ended with me surrendering and getting in the car, no matter how many times I tried to explain to him that he was dead and I had a new life. The more I unpacked my pain into neat text in the waking world, the more it flooded my

222

mind, as if I had opened the floodgates that had kept me par-
tially sane for the last five years. I had to face myself – and feel
the feelings – all while trapped in the house, responsible for the
wellbeing of my next of kin.

I thought of everything I had learned over the last thirty years.
It was apparent that the more things had changed for me, the
more it had remained the same in my head. I was forever tar-
nished by a whole community that had failed me as a girlchild.

And the more things remained toxic and confusing in the
world.

I have no conclusions, or profound words of wisdom to impart
to people in the very pressure-filled final chapter of my book.
Actually, profoundly, I am only on the first chapter of my real life.

# Glossary

**afdak** – in the case of a bakkie, this is a canopy; in the case of a
house, this is an 'overhang'

**afshowerag** – adjective: show-off

**Aspoestertjie** – literally Cinderella of the fairytale; also a
woman of a lower calibre, not worthy of Prince Charming

**bevoeled** – felt up, fondled

**bra/brasse** – friend(s)

**bymekaar** – together (as in a couple); also, to hook up

**dala** – to make a move/make moves

**dik** – very; also, fat, big

**dik lippe** – big lips

**erg** – gross, disgusting; also, hectic

**fokkol** – fuck all, nothing

**gees** – to be an expert

**gevriet** – face

**gham/gam** – 'ghetto' Coloured, a lower calibre of Coloured,
often used negatively or with disdain

**gran** – to like

**hocks** – hopscotch

**hos (also hosh)** – a greeting, like 'aweh'; in certain contexts, it
can be used as a warning or an acclamation that someone
is crossing a line, in the same way that Coloured people
sometimes use the expression 'Hallo!'

**houte** – a hard-on, an erection

**iets/ietsie** – something, a little something

**jas** – mad, crazy, angry, impressive

**jol/jolling** – to hook up/hooking up; also, a party

**jy/jy's** – you/you are

**kaare** – lies, intricate lies

**kin (pl. kinnes)** – girl, girlfriend

**klom** – as in klomp; a lot

**koekie** – vagina

**koppel** – to organise, to meet up

**kroon** – money

**kyn** – i.e. 'What kyn?' – What's wrong? What's up?

**lam** – to chill, relax

**los kin** – a sexually loose woman, a whore

**los kind** – an illegitimate child

**lus** – to crave, to feel like

**lyf** – body

**maarts** – literally 'to march', to leave

**miang stokkies** – incense sticks

**motchie** – girlfriend, wife

**naai** – noun: an asshole; verb: to fuck, to have sex with; also, 'no'

**ougat** – a precocious child, old fashioned, to have sexual inclinations

**paar** – a few, more than once

**party ou** – party guy, the life of the party

**permy** – always

**piel** – penis

**pla** – to worry, to bother

**poes** – vagina

**reg** – literally 'right'; adjective: hot, good-looking

226

**sien jy?** – you see?

**smaak** – to like someone (romantically), to have the desire to do something, i.e. I smaak to dance

**smokkie** – an illegal bottle store (different to a shebeen, which is a yaart)

**stil** – quiet

**sturvy** – bougie, fancy

**taani** – mother

**tapyt** – plastic flooring, vinyl, linoleum

**tik'd it out** – sold it for tik

**tjunk** – also tjank, to cry

**tollie** – penis

**trekked** – as in 'the dop trekked' – the alcohol kicked in/took effect

**trot manskap** – men who don't have cars, men who walk everywhere

**uitgerek** – spoilt, damaged goods, stretched out

**vuilgat** – see vullis

**vullis** – a piece of shit, a dirt bag

**vry** – to kiss, to make out

**warme klappe** – painful smacks

**wys** – to know, to show

**yous** – you guys

# Thank you

I am filled to the brim with gratitude for so many people who were integral to this writing journey. But I will keep my wordcount low because long winded speeches are self-indulgent, no matter what the subject matter. To start, I want to thank my husband, Riyaahd Fife, for the late nights of taking over everything while I was hidden away in my writing room amidst mostly unfolded laundry and tears of frustration. I appreciate you deeply. Thank you, Aimee Carelse, for having faith in my story. None of this would be possible without you. Thank you Mom and Dad, Sidney and Sarah Genever, for all your help and encouragement – and taking the kids when my mind just couldn't handle writing, working, parenting and being manic all at once. Thank you to my friends who read my ramblings at all hours of the day and night when I needed a sounding board and honestly just some inspiration to keep going: Raisa Fisher, Farhaanah Ayub, Fozia Jacobs, Bronwyn Davids, Celest Dreyer and Hayley Jacobs, and of course, my entire WolfKraft Productions family who have my back through everything. And there are so many more of you who I appreciate who offered me a kind word or hot beverage instead of a hug during this time – I acknowledge you and hold you in high esteem.

CPSIA information can be obtained
at www.ICGtesting.com
Printed in the USA
LVHW081722211021
700931LV00025BA/811